THE PRINCIPAL NATIONS OF INDIA

THE PRINCIPAL NATIONS OF INDIA

COMPILED FROM HUNTER, DALTON, CALDWELL, CUST, LATHAM, AND OTHERS.

GYAN

Published by

GYAN

Gyan Publishing House
5, Ansari Road
Daryaganj, New Delhi-110002
Phone: 011-47034999, 9811692060
E-mail: books@gyanbooks.com

Distribution Network
gyanbooks.com
India, USA, Canada, UK, Australia, France

ISBN : 978-81-212-1431-5 (PB)
First Published, 1903

2nd Impression 2021

Printed at: Gyan Press, Delhi.

The
Principal Nations of India
Compiled from: Hunter, Dalton, Caldwell, Cust, Latham, and Others.

THE PRINCIPAL NATIONS OF INDIA

COMPILED FROM HUNTER, DALTON, CALDWELL, CUST, LATHAM, AND OTHERS.

THE CHRISTIAN LITERATURE SOCIETY FOR INDIA:
LONDON AND MADRAS.

4TH ED.] 1903.

CONTENTS.

NOTE.—The following works were chiefly used in this compilation:

Hunter's *Gazetteer of India*. 14 Vols. Trübner.
Dalton's *Ethnology of Bengal*. Calcutta.
Caldwell's *Comparative Grammar of the Dravidian Languages*. Trübner.
Cust's *Modern Languages of the East Indies*. Trübner.
Latham's *Comparative Philology*. Walton and Maberly.

THE NATIONS OF INDIA.

INTRODUCTION.

WE ought to know something about the different nations inhabiting the large country of India in which we live. This little book is intended to give an account of the principal of them. Upwards of a hundred languages and dialects are spoken in India; so that only a few nations can be described, and even these, in most cases, very briefly.

The position and size of the country may first be noticed. India forms the central peninsula of Southern Asia. It lies between the Himalaya Mountains on the north, and the Indian Ocean on the south. On the east it is bounded by Burma and the Bay of Bengal; on the west by the Arabian Sea, Baluchistan and Afghanistan.

Its greatest length and breadth are each about 1,800 miles. The entire area is about 1½ millions of square miles. It is rather more than one-third of the size of Europe. Its area, compared with all the land on the globe, is in about the proportion of half an anna to a rupee. The population of India in 1901 was about 28 crores. Of every six persons in the world, one is a native of India.

Before describing the nations of India as they exist at present, a short account will be given of the different races by which it has been successively entered.

Aborigines.—Who first peopled India, and where they came from, is not yet known with certainty. Sir George Campbell supposes them to have been Negritos, a small dark negro-like race, spread over the whole of the Australian and Indian Archipelago. They are found in a comparatively pure state in the Andaman islands.

In the Narbada Valley rough flint weapons have been discovered, probably relics of the earliest inhabitants.

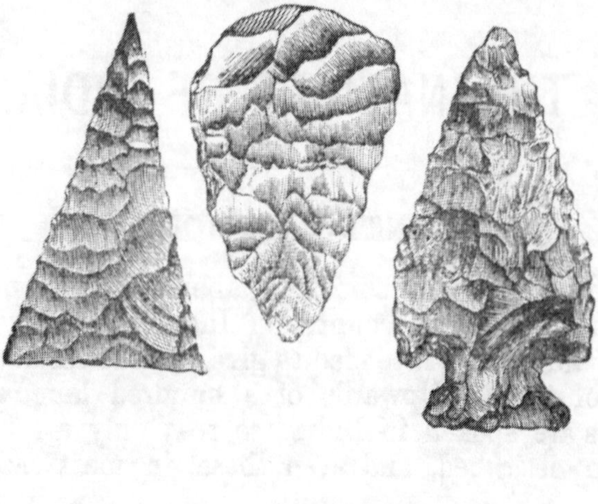

ROUGH FLINT WEAPONS.

In the Central Provinces and elsewhere polished axes and other stone implements have been dug up, similar to those found in Northern Europe. These show a little advance in civilization.

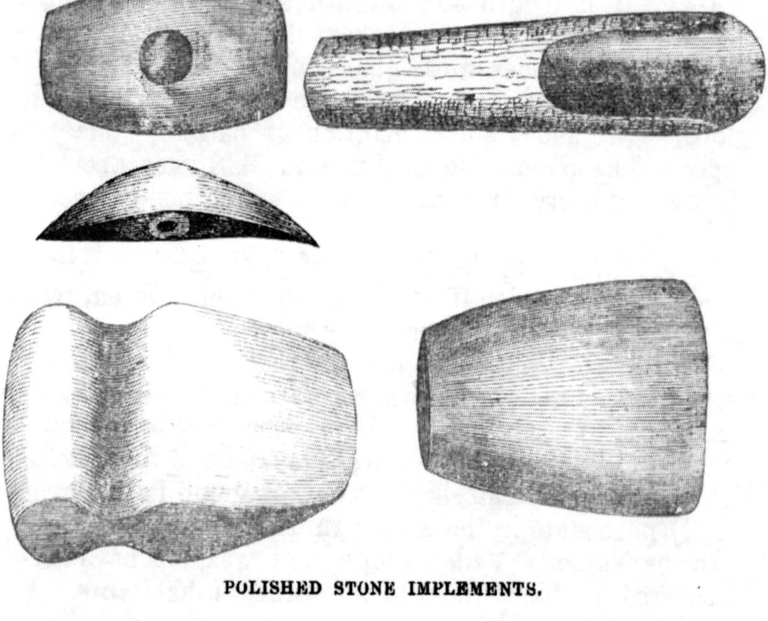

POLISHED STONE IMPLEMENTS.

There were probably, at a later period, other tribes, like some of those in India at present, who knew how to make

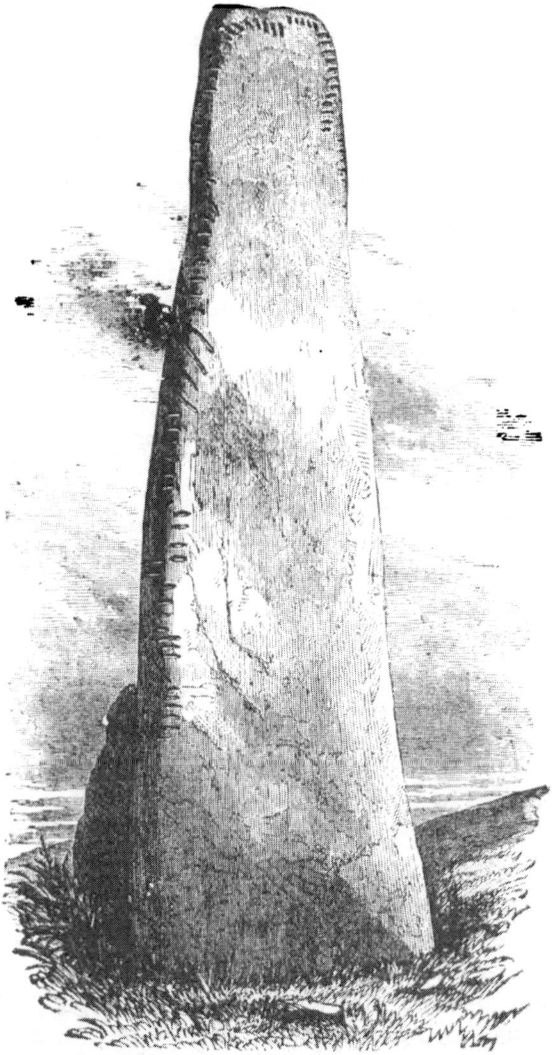

MEMORIAL GRAVE STONE.

round pots of earthenware, not inelegant in shape, who fought with iron weapons, and wore ornaments of copper and gold. They left no written records; indeed the use of letters or of the simplest marks was to them unknown. The sole works of their hands which have come down to us are rude stone circles, and the upright slabs and mounds beneath which, like the primitive peoples of Europe, they buried their dead. Coins of imperial Rome have been dug up from their graves. Some of them must, therefore, have lived within the Christian era. Indeed, there are tribes, both in Northern and Southern India, which still preserve the same customs.

Races from the North-East.—At an early period some tribes, which had dwelt in Central Asia side by side with the forefathers of the Mongolians and the Chinese, crossed over to India by the north-eastern passes, and spread along the base of the Himalayas and their north-eastern offshoots. The Kolarians appear also to have entered India by the same route, and to have proceeded in a south-westerly direction. The Santals are one of the most numerous of the Kolarian races.

Dravidians from the North-West.—The ancestors of the principal nations of Southern India appear to have entered India from the north-west. It would seem as if the two streams, the Kolarians from the north-east and the Dravidians from the north-west, had crossed each other in Central India. The Dravidians proved the stronger, broke up the Kolarians, and thrust aside their fragments to the east and west. The Dravidians then went forward in a mighty body to the south.

Entry of the Aryans from the North-West.—The ancestors of the Aryan nations lived together at a remote period, probably in the highlands of Central Asia. When they increased in number so that their original home was unable to support them, they emigrated in bands. Some went westward towards the setting sun, and peopled North-Western Asia and Europe. They have been the prominent actors in the great drama of history. The Hindus, perhaps after seeing their brethren depart, turned their faces eastward, and advanced towards the valley of the Indus. They marched in a large body, with their families, their servants, their cattle. India was probably entered by the mountain passes near Peshawar. Rivers were forded at conveniently shallow places, or, if deep, they were crossed in boats.

The greater part of India was then covered with forest, with scattered villages and towns belonging to the earlier settlers, who were of a dark complexion and spoke a strange language. The Aryans had the pride of race in an extravagant degree, showing great contempt for and hatred of the other nations with whom they came in contact. The new-comers from the north prided themselves on their fair complexion, and the Sanskrit word for 'colour' (*varna*) came to mean 'race' or 'caste.' They called the aborigines the 'black skin;' and as their noses were not so large as theirs, they were described as 'goat nosed' or 'noseless.' One of the Vedic singers praises his own "beautiful nosed" gods. The Vedic hymns also describe the primitive tribes as "disturbers of sacrifices," "gross feeders of flesh," "raw-eaters." They were called *Dasyus*, a word supposed to mean *enemies*. So many of them were enslaved, that the word *dasa* was afterwards applied to a servant.

Some of the Dasyus were like the Bhils or other wild tribes of India at present; others had a partial civilization. In several of the Vedic hymns the wealth of the Dasyus is mentioned, *e.g.*: "Subdue the might of the Dasa; may we through Indra divide his collected wealth." They had forts and cities. "Indra and Agni, by one effort together ye have shattered 90 forts belonging to the Dasyus." "O Indra, impetuous, thou didst shatter by thy bolt 99 cities for Puru."

The Aryas, as they advanced, gradually established themselves in the forests, fields, and villages of the aborigines. The latter contended as bravely as they could against their invaders. Their black complexion, barbarous habits, rude speech, and savage yells during their night attacks, made the Aryas speak of them as demons.

The Aryas were the more powerful. The Dasyus were either driven before them or were reduced to slavery. The first great distinction in India was between the white and dark races, the conquerors and the conquered, the freeman and the slave. One of the earliest aboriginal tribes brought under subjection was called Sudras, and the name was extended to the whole race.

The war of invasion lasted for centuries, nor were the aborigines, as a whole, subjugated at any period.

The Indus is the great river of the Vedas; the Ganges is only twice mentioned. By degrees the Aryas spread eastward till they reached the Saraswati, which was the boundary in Vedic times.

In course of time the Aryans went eastward to Bengal, and southwards toward the north of the Deccan. Though the great Dravidian nations in the south accepted largely the Brahmanical system, they were not incorporated with the Aryans as in the north.

Parsis.—The Parsis came from Persia. When it was conquered by the Muhammadans, the Parsis were persecuted on account of their religions and some of them took refuge in India.

Muhammadans.—The Arabs, in 711 A.D., seized part of Sind; but the following century, it was regained by the Hindus. For many years afterwards the Muhammadans did not think of invading India. In 977 Jaipal, Maharaja of Lahore, attacked Sabaktigin of Ghazni, but he was defeated. Mahmud of Ghazni, son of Sabaktigin, is well known for his numerous invasions of India. Muhammad Ghori may be regarded as the founder of the Muhammadan power in India. At his death in 1206, the greater part of Northern India was subject to him. In 1526, Baber, the founder of the Mogul Empire, invaded India, and for about two centuries the dynasty which he founded was the ruling power. This contributed greatly to the spread of Muhammadanism, which is now professed by rather more than one in five of the inhabitants of India.

Portuguese.—Vasco da Gama landed at Calicut in 1498. Other expeditions followed, and soon the Portuguese had settlements from Surat in the west to Chittagong in the east.

English.—In 1600, towards the close of the reign of Queen Elizabeth, the East India Company was formed for the purpose of trade. Their first settlement was at Masulipatam in 1620. Madras was purchased in 1639. Three villages were bought in 1698 on the banks of the Hugli on which Calcutta now stands. The aid of the English was sought in war by the Indian Princes, and by degrees they made themselves the paramount power in the country.

Other European nations came to India in smaller numbers, as the Dutch, French, and Danes.

Some of the principal nations at the present time will now be described, beginning with the Bengalis.

A BENGALI CHRISTIAN AND HIS DAUGHTERS.

THE BENGALIS.

Next to the Hindi-speaking tribes, the Bengalis form the largest nationality in India. They number nearly four crores of the inhabitants of India, one in every seven is a Bengali.

Country.—Ancient Bengal formed one of the five outlying kingdoms of Aryan India. The name applies strictly to the country stretching south-east from Bhagalpur to the sea; but it was afterwards extended.

The most distinctive feature of Bengal is its rivers. It consists chiefly of two broad river valleys. By the western one, the Ganges brings down the waters of Northern India. The eastern valley contains the lower course of the Brahmaputra, after it has drained the table-land of Tibet. In Northern Bengal the plains are diversified by hills thrown out by the great mountain chains. Near the centre of the province the main channels of the rivers, after meeting, throw off branches, right and left. The diminished force of their currents renders them unable to carry along the silt which they have brought down. The streams therefore deposit their burden in their channels and upon their banks, so that by degrees their beds rise above the level of the surrounding country. During the rains they overflow their banks, leaving their silt upon the adjacent flats which are thus fertilised. As the rivers creep farther down the Delta, they become more and more sluggish. The last scene is a wilderness of swamp, amid whose solitude the net work of channels merges into the sea.

Bengal is chiefly one large rice-producing plain; but oilseeds, jute, indigo, sugar, and tobacco, are also raised in considerable quantities. The numerous rivers yield a large supply of fish which forms an important article of food.

The Bengalis.—Mr. Beverley thus describes them :—

"In Bengal Proper we have a people physically distinct from any other race in India. Whether, on the one hand, they are to be attributed to climatic influences and the natural characteristics of the country, or, on the other, to the great infusion of aboriginal blood, that people presents national peculiarities sufficient to identify it in any part of the world. Living amid a network of rivers and morasses, and nourished on a watery rice diet, the semi-amphibious Bengali in appearance belongs to a weak and puny race, yet he is able to endure an amount of exposure to which the up-country Hindustani would soon fall a victim. In active pursuits the Bengali is timid and slothful, but in intellect he is subtle and sharpwitted; and these latter qualities, combined with a plodding industry and a natural fondness for sedentary employments, have carried him into Government offices all over the country, and raised him to some of the highest judicial posts in the land. Besides inhabiting the province of Bengal Proper, Bengalis are found in considerable numbers in the border districts, such as Purneah, the Sonthal Pergunnahs, Maunbhoom, and Goalpara."*

Language.—Bengali belongs to the northern family of languages. The character is the same as the Nagri, but rounded for greater facility in writing. There is a fondness for the sound *o*: thus Manu becomes Monu.

BENGALI.

কেননা ঈশ্বর জগতের প্রতি এমত প্রেম করিলেন, যে আপনার
অদ্বিতীয় পুত্রকে দান করিলেন; যেন তাঁহাতে বিশ্বাসকারি
প্রত্যেক জন বিনষ্ট না হইয়া অনন্ত জীবন পায়।

Bengali and Oriya contain a larger proportion of words purely Sanskrit in form than the other languages of the northern family. Beames, in his "Comparative Grammar of the Modern Aryan Languages of India," complains that Bengali words, in the book language, have been replaced by their Sanskrit forms; so that bad Sanskrit is sometimes written instead of good Bengali. Obsolete grammatical forms have to some extent been revived. In consequence of this, some books are almost unintelligible to the common people.

Of late years there has been a change for the better.

* Report of Census of Bengal, 1872, p. 152.

Newspapers, treating of everyday life, could not well be written in the stilted book form, and they have led to greater simplicity of language in other kinds of literature. In the dramas, which are now numerous, the speakers use the forms of speech current among the classes whom they represent.

Muhammadans mix with Bengali a number of Arabic and Persian words. Their language is called Musalman-Bengali.

Rural Life.—The great bulk of the people are employed in agriculture. They live chiefly in villages. There are few large towns in Bengal.

BENGALI COTTAGE.

Bengali cottages are usually built of mud, or mat-bamboos, and straw. They are generally raised above the ground to keep them dry when the country is flooded. The

BENGAL PADDY-POUNDER.

roof is of thatch, and sloped to shed the rain easily. The flat mud roofs of the Upper Provinces, where the rainfall is slight, would not do in Bengal. The clustered cottages are generally hidden among trees.

The furniture, as in other parts of India, is generally very scanty. Paddy is not husked by a pestle, but by means of an instrument moved by the foot.

In some parts every house has its canoe, as the country is under water during the rainy season. Some of the canoes are so small that a man can carry one on his head; others are larger, and have a kind of covering as in the picture below.

RIVER BOAT.

VILLAGE MARKET OR HAT.

Bengal being a land of villages, markets are a necessity. When one is held, canoes come laden with produce.

Numerous bridges are required over the small creeks. They are often made of bamboo, as they can be so easily put up and taken down. Only Bengalis with their bare feet can walk over them without slipping.

What is called the "Permanent Settlement" prevails in Bengal. Hence, although the value of the land has greatly increased, Government cannot raise the land tax. The Zemindars raise the rents, and the ryots pay; but the increase goes to the Zemindars.

Many of the Zemindars have sublet their lands to middlemen, who, in their turn, sublet to others. Ryots sometimes pay their rents to several different landlords.

BAMBOO BRIDGE.

City Life.—Every morning and evening almost all the main streets of Calcutta leading to the business part of the city are thronged with numbers of Bengalis, dressed in white, with bare heads, making for or returning from their offices either by tramway, in *tika gharis*, or on foot. Some are good copyists, others clever accountants, while a few are correspondence clerks. Many families are thus maintained.

Other Bengalis are shopkeepers or merchants; some are lawyers; a few have risen to high position as judges.

The Bengalis, like other nations, have their good and bad qualities. Their faults have been freely exposed by some of themselves. One of them says:—

"In the progressive development of the Bengali character, the volubility of the tongue may be precipitated into energy of action; but, in the meantime, its prevailing characteristic is rapid talk. One of our national poets, describing the character of a certain individual, says, '*He was mountain-like in words, in deeds mustard-seed-like.*' It is not too much to say that in those words is comprehended the predominant feature of our national character. We have no doubt that, under the influences of a sound education, of improved social institutions, and of a pure faith, the national character of the Bengali will undergo a glorious transformation; but, in the meantime, its chief characteristic is words, words, words."

Few things have done more to corrupt the young men of Calcutta than the rage for theatrical performances in which prostitutes are actresses. The public display of their charms leads to private engagements. A vigorous effort should be made to put an end to this disgraceful state of things.

In Bengal, as in some other parts of India, an inordinate degree of attention is given to politics. The *Indian Mirror*, a Calcutta daily native paper, says :—

"We are now talking politics to death; and though we are ourselves always in the thick of politics, we must confess that politics has positively become the bane of our society, because we are giving this undue prominence to it to the neglect and at the sacrifice of other questions, in which our present progress and future welfare are materially involved."*

The mischievous effects are most felt upon the young. *The Hindu* quotes the following :—

"A Calcutta contemporary advocates the advisability of checking the unhealthy growth of political agitation amongst schoolboys and students. . . . It strongly contends that, if this course is not followed, something must be done to check the mendacious scurrility that is sapping the foundation of the society which, in a few years, will take the place of that which now constitutes the educated society of Bengal."†

The Bengalis have passed through different phases. Forty years ago they were the leaders in social and other reforms. Under the influence of false patriotism, there is a reactionary movement among some. Everything Indian

* Quoted in *Concord*, Oct. 3, 1886. † 31st October, 1885.

is right, because it is Indian; that anything is foreign, is regarded as a sufficient condemnation. Intelligent Bengalis see the folly of this. As one of them remarked at a public meeting, "*Rationality* should not be sacrificed for *Nationality*." The great question should be, Is a custom right or wrong in itself?

The Bengalee gave the following caution:—

"We attach the greatest importance to the cause of social reform in Bengal. Let it not be said that the Bengalee Babu is blatant enough when he has to cry down the Government, but that he shrinks from the sacrifice which social reform would impose upon him. An imputation of this kind, if allowed to be made with a show of reason, would be fatal to the cause of all progress—political as well as social."

The *Indian Messenger* does not fear that the reactionary movement will obstruct the cause of reform; but regrets it because it "will tell seriously upon the intellectual honesty of the rising generation, and give a premium to hypocrisy and self-satisfaction."

On the other hand, some of the most distinguished Indians in modern times have been Bengalis. They include men noted for their learning, like Dr. Rajendralala Mitra, Dr. Krishna Mohun Banerjea, and several writers on Hindu law; journalists like Kristo Das Pal, and social reformers like Pandit Vidyasagar. Above all, Bengal has produced the greatest Indian religious reformers of the century, as Rammohun Roy and Keshub Chunder Sen.

Religion.—It is estimated that of the Hindus in Bengal about three-fourths are Saktis. The wife of Siva, under the names of Durga and Kali, is chiefly worshipped. She is represented as a black woman with four hands, wearing a necklace of skulls and dancing on the body of Siva. After her victory over the giant, she danced for joy so furiously, that the earth trembled beneath her weight. As she did not stop when Siva asked her, he lay down among the slain. She continued dancing till she caught sight of her husband under her feet, upon which she put out her tongue.

DURGA.

The Kalika Purana says: "By a human sacrifice, attended by the forms laid down, Devi remains gratified for a thousand years." Dr. Rajendralala Mitra says: "There is scarcely a respectable house in all Bengal the mistress of which has not, at one time or other, shed her blood under the notion of satisfying the goddess by the operation."

The *Durga Puja* is the chief festival in Bengal. It is intended to celebrate the victory over the Asura Sumbha, who attacked Durga under the form of a buffalo. Hence the goddess is called Mahisha-mardini. The story of the fight is so extravagant, that any one except a Hindu would laugh at it for its absurdity.

The first part of the festival is the *bodhana*, or the awaking of the goddess, who is supposed to have been sleeping for the past two months. She is invited to come to the house, and dwell in the image which has been prepared for her. After this the *pran pratishta* ceremony is performed. For three days the worship is continued. Offerings and sacrifices are made. Kids are usually the victims; but, in some cases, buffaloes. The following prayer is offered: "Grant me, O lady, long life, fair name, good fortune, sons, riches, and all other desires."

On the afternoon of the fourth day, the goddess is supposed to take leave of the image, which is afterwards thrown into the river.

"In the gaiety of children released from their books, in the pleasures of well-earned rest, in the hospitalities of brotherhood, in the courtesies of friendship, in the joys of family gatherings, in the happy greetings of loving hearts long separated, we can all rejoice." It is sad, however, that this innocent pleasure should be connected with a festival to celebrate a lie, and with thanksgiving to an idol instead of the great Creator and Giver of all good. The *Indian Messenger* has the following remarks:—

"The spectacle of nearly a whole country, ignorant of the spiritual worship of the true God, and rejoicing in the bloody worship of idols, is sickening enough; but far more sickening and melancholy than this worship of idols by believers in popular Hinduism, ignorant of the spiritual worship of God, is the spectacle of educated men, convinced of the falsity of idolatry, rejoicing and taking part in it.

"All this cannot but make every sincere lover of truth sorry for the educated classes of this country. English education, in enfranchising their intellects, has not enfranchised their conscience; has not made them truth-loving and honest. It has, on the contrary, taught them an ingenuity which can defend any amount of moral cowardice and effeminacy by plausible arguments. There are not wanting men among the educated classes who are not ashamed,—who, at any rate, profess not to be ashamed,—of the life of compromise with idolatry and superstition which they are living."

Chaitanya, a Brahman born at Naddia in 1485 A.D., is

largely worshipped in Bengal as an incarnation of Krishna. Prostitutes generally profess to be his disciples, as being expelled from their own caste, it is only by this means that they can obtain funeral rites. Chaitanya is an example of the way in which the Hindus manufacture their gods.

Half the Bengalis are Muhammadans. In some districts they form three-fourths of the population. Most of them were originally low-caste Hindus who professed the religion of their conquerors to rise in the social scale. Fifty years ago they were Muhammadans merely in name, the majority of them being unable to repeat even their creed. They were a mongrel breed of circumcised low-caste Hindus. Now they are somewhat better instructed.

Kiernander, the first Protestant Missionary to Bengal, came to Calcutta from Madras in 1758. He built the old Mission Church in Mission Row. Carey landed at Calcutta in 1793. In 1799, four missionaries followed. As the British Government was then hostile to missionaries in India, Carey and his brethren took shelter in the Danish Settlement of Serampore. It was not till 1813 that India was officially thrown open to missionaries. The Rev. Alexander Duff, who arrived in Calcutta in 1830, gave a great impulse to English education. In 1901 the number of Protestant Bengali Christians was about 33,000.

Rammohun Roy, chiefly through intercourse with missionaries, was led to seek the religious reformation of his countrymen. Keshub Chunder Sen for some time laboured zealously in the same direction; but latterly his tendency was towards Hinduism. His followers, since his death, have been much divided among themselves.

The Sadharan Brahma Samaj is simply theistic.

Literature and the Press.—Bengali literature is comparatively modern. The Brahmans wrote only in Sanskrit, the vernacular being despised as fit merely for "demons and women." The Muhammadan conquerors encouraged only Persian. Ram Comul Sen says in the preface to his Dictionary: "The composition of bibliographical and historical works in Bengali commenced on the appearance of Chaitanya in Nadiya, about 307 years ago; his disciples wrote various books on the doctrines of the Vaishnava sect."

The most ancient specimen of printing in Bengali is Halhed's Grammar, printed at Hugli in 1778. The types for this grammar were prepared by Sir C. Wilkins. He instructed a native blacksmith, named Panchanan, in type-cutting, and all the native knowledge of type-cutting was derived from him.

The life of Raja Pratapaditya, the last king of Sagar, published in 1801 at Serampore, is said by the Rev. J. Long to have been one of the first works written in Bengali prose. It is half Persian, half Bengali. *The Friend of India* gave in 1820 with no small satisfaction a list of 27 Bengali books issued from the native presses during the previous ten years. "Fifteen thousand volumes printed and sold among the natives within the last ten years, a phenomenon to which the country has been a stranger since the formation of the first, the incommunicable letters of the Vedas!"

The number of works published of late years has been very large, though the utility of many of them may be doubted.

The Press.—Calcutta has some of the best and worst papers in India. *The Hindu Patriot*, when under the late Hon. Kristo Das Pal, was, on the whole, admirably conducted. *The Indian Messenger* at present occupies a very high place from its fairness, moral tone, and enlightened views generally. But there are others of a different character. The *Indian Mirror* had the following remarks in 1874, and things have not greatly improved since then:

"Any one who will go through the weekly reports on the Native papers, cannot help thinking that in the current vocabulary of our contemporaries, education means the loss of respect for the Government; public spirit is synonymous with empty bluster; patriotism is hatred of Englishmen, and impartiality is gross abuse."

The Indian Messenger says: "The misfortune of our province is that its vaunted enlightenment is exhibited more in carping and captious criticism than in wholesome activity."

The idea of a patriot, with some, is the man who brags most of the "ancient glories of India," and most depreciates modern progress; who defends every national belief and custom, and denounces everything foreign; and who most vilifies the English character and the English administration.

The late Kristo Das Pal characterised those who performed *prayaschitta* on their return from Europe as "imbecile swallowers of penitential pills." The *Amrita Bazar Patrika* holds them up to admiration for their heroism and moral courage! It has been remarked that this illustrates "how possible it is even for men claiming respectability to debase themselves before the whole world, and for them and their friends to glory in their shame."

The people generally are conservative and anti-reformers, and the journals that support their views have the largest circulation. The *Bangabasi*, it is said, has an issue of 20,000 weekly.

Some years ago the late Sir H. S. Maine said that there was no greater or more destructive mistake than to defend false beliefs by sophistical arguments. Mr. Gladstone remarked: "I do not believe you can do a greater injury to your country than to flatter it." Happily there is an enlightened minority in Bengal who consider it the worst treachery to call evil good, to allow error and wrong to remain unchecked, and to stir up nationality against nationality.

THE ASSAMESE.

The Assamese inhabit a long narrow valley, watered by the Brahmaputra. In features and in history they are distinct from the great body of the Hindus, though in recent times they have adopted the Brahmanical religion. Assam formed part of the ancient kingdom of Kamrup, whose capital was Gauhati. It was overthrown by Muhammadan invaders in the 15th century. The Kochs, an aboriginal tribe, afterwards founded a kingdom, at one time as extensive as that of Kamrup. The Maharaja of Kuch Behar still represents the main line of this dynasty. The Ahams, a Shan tribe of the same stock as the Siamese, subdued the Kochs. The Ahams, in danger of being exterminated by the Burmese, asked the English to interfere. Assam was annexed to British India in 1824 after the first Burmese war.

According to the Census of 1881, Assamese was spoken by about 14 lakhs. Some consider Assamese a mere dialect of Bengali, but this is denied by the Assamese, who are not willing to abandon their language. It abounds with words of Sanskrit origin. Cust says that the pronunciation corresponds rather with Hindi than with Bengali. Good prose is found in the historical works written about two or three centuries ago.

Mr. Beverley thus describes the Assamese:

"At the other extreme of Bengal we find another distinct nationality in the Assamese,—a race speaking a language very similar to Bengali, but largely tainted in descent by the mixture of Indo-Chinese blood. The valley of the Brahmaputra has been the scene of frequent revolutions, by which one tribe has succeeded to another, and each has left its traces on the character and physique of the present inhabitants. The purest Assamese, it is believed, are the Ahams of the Sibsagar District, but few have kept their lineage undefiled; and the present inhabitants of the provinces may be described as a mongrel race with Aham, Chutiya, Koch, Bodo, and Aryan blood in their veins. They are a proud, haughty and indolent people: the use of opium, to which they are addicted, having, it is said, an injurious influence upon the national character."*

Some efforts have recently been made to lessen the use of opium among the Assamese.

The country is being opened up by steam navigation and railways.

The Province of Assam is occupied by several hill tribes, two or three of which will be described.

* Bengal Census of 1872, p. 145.

NAGAS.

THE NAGAS.

The Nagas, 100,000 in number, occupy the hills to the north-east of Cachar. Their features are like the Burmese, they have flat noses, and high cheek bones. Their dress consists of a dark blue kilt, ornamented with cowry shells. The most coveted decoration is a neck collar, made of goat's hair dyed red, fringed with the long scalps of slain enemies. The national weapons are a spear, a shield, and a *dao*, or bill hook. When proceeding on a foray, they carry a large stock of pointed bamboos, a few inches in length, intended to be stuck in the ground, to delay the pursuit of an enemy. They are brave in war, but also treacherous and vindictive. If one of their number is slain, nothing will pacify them till revenge is taken.

The Nagas are very superstitious in the matter of omens. All their ceremonies and sacrifices are intended to appease the wrath of numerous evil spirits.

Their funeral ceremonies are very singular. When death occurs from lingering illness, a platform is raised within the house on which the body is placed and watched day and night. When the illness has been short, the platform is erected in a neighbouring jungle, and the corpse folded in cloths, is placed on it and left to decay. When six months have expired, the funeral ceremonies are performed. A large gathering of the friends takes place; music and dancing are continued through an entire day and night, with laments and death songs, brandishing of spears, and imprecations of the evil spirit, who, they suppose, had taken away their friend.

THE MISHMIS.

The Mishmis are a hill tribe on the eastern frontier of Assam, supposed to be connected with the aborigines of Yunan in Western China. They are a short, sturdy race, with a fair complexion and features of a softened Mongolian type. Their dress is made of striped cloth; their armour consists of helmet, sword, and spear; the women wear ornaments of beads and silver. Some of the tribes turn up the hair and tie it in a knot, whilst others are closely cropped. They are very filthy, as they never wash.

The Mishmis are traders. Every man among them will either buy or sell. They are also blacksmiths and forge their own spear heads, though they buy as well. They are skilful in making suspension bridges.

The Mishmi hamlets consist of a few houses, sometimes of only one; but each house is capable of holding all the members of a family, besides numerous slaves and retainers. One of the chiefs had a house built of bamboos raised high from the ground, divided into 12 compartments, and containing 100 men, women and children. Another house had 20 compartments.

Polygamy is common; the limit to the number of wives being the means of the husband. For each wife he must give so many head of cattle. The women mix with the men, and join them in every labour but that of the chase.

The Mishmis are rich in flocks and herds. They have large herds of the fine hill ox. They are not used for agricultural purposes or for their milk, but on great occasions one is slaughtered and eaten, and they are given in exchange for brides. They are allowed to remain almost in a wild state, roving through the forests as they please, but they are fed with salt by their master; and when he calls, they know his voice.

Women are highly priced and a large family of daughters is a fortune to any man. Poor younger sons have to work hard before they can take a wife to a home of their own. On payment of part of the purchase-money, the youth may marry and visit his wife at his father's house, though she and her children can never leave it till all is paid.

A chief's house is strangely ornamented. Long poles of bamboo are hung with the blackened smoke-dried skulls of all the animals with which the owner had ever feasted his friends and retainers. He is proud of them as showing his hospitality. When a chief dies the body is burnt after two days, and the ashes are collected and placed in a miniature house erected close to the family residence. The skulls are all cleared away and buried near the burial place of the chief himself. Then his son will take pride in filling the house afresh. It is considered mean for a chief to retain in his show room the skulls of animals killed by his predecessors.

When trouble comes upon a Mishmi, he sacrifices fowls or pigs to the evil spirits, and places the branch of a tree over his door to inform strangers that his house is under a temporary ban, and that it must not be entered.

A Mishmi, when told of a good spirit who ruled all the demons, said: "Ah! you English people must be very happy in having such a good and powerful demon in your country. The Mishmis are very unfortunate. We are everywhere surrounded by demons; they live in the rivers, mountains and trees; they walk about in the dark and live in the winds. We are constantly suffering from them."

THE GAROS.

The Garos, about 140,000 in number, inhabit the western end of the chain of mountains between the Surma and Brahmaputra valleys.

The Garos are a robust active race, of about the middle height, and of a dark brown colour. Their cheek bones are prominent, noses broad, lips thick, ears large, and eyes of a light brown colour. The men are remarkable for deficiency of beard, whatever hair grows on the face being carefully plucked out. The hair of the head of both sexes is never cut, but either tied up in a knot, or kept off the face by means of a piece of cloth. The dress of the men consists merely of a strip of cotton cloth, about a yard and a half in length, which is passed round the waist and between the legs, and then tied at the back. The dress of the women differs only in being slightly more extensive. In addition, both sexes carry a small blanket, usually made from the bark of a tree. This is manufactured by steeping the bark in water, beating it out, and afterwards drying it well in the sun. Both men and women are inordinately fond of personal ornaments. The males wear three or four brass ear-rings, and as many bead necklaces as they can afford. Men of hereditary rank wear an iron or brass armlet above the elbow, and a peculiar ornament round the head, which consists of brass plates connected by a string. This lost, it is said, can only be assumed by one who has slain an enemy in battle.

The women wear, besides necklaces of glass and bell-metal, beads and ear-rings of enormous size and weight. It is a coveted mark of distinction to have the lobe of the ear altogether torn away by the strain thus caused, in which case the ear-rings are suspended from a string passed over the top of the head.

The weapons of the Garos consist of spear, sword and shield. The sword, which is peculiar to those hills, is a two-edged instrument with an abrupt point, the blade and handle forming one piece. Besides being a weapon, it is used in every variety of domestic and agricultural purpose. The shield is composed of thin strips of bamboo, ingeniously worked together, so as to be proof against a spear-thrust. In the back of the shield is a receptacle for bamboo spikes to block the way of a shoeless enemy.

In food the Garos eat not only beef and pork, but also tigers, dogs, snakes and frogs. Their staple diet is rice, and their drink rice beer. Milk they altogether eschew, as do all the hill tribes between the Surma and Brahmaputra. They are great smokers of tobacco, but touch no intoxicating drug.

Like the Himalayan tribes, the Nairs of Travancore, and the Todas of the Nilgiris, the wife is regarded as the head of the family, and through her the descent of property is traced. According to this system, where in full force, a woman is the lawful wife of a family of brothers, and a man's property descends, not to his own, but to his sister's children. Among the Garos property still descends through the females, and the sons receive nothing, but have to look to the family into which they marry for their advancement in life. In no case is a son allowed to bring him a wife and live with his parents.

The dead among the Garos are burned, and the ashes buried near the hut door. At the time of cremation, dogs are sacrificed in order that they may direct the spirit on its way. Up to a very recent period, human victims were offered on the occasion of the death of a chief. If no slaves were available, a raid was made into the plains to bring back heads. The skulls were hung up in their houses, and he who had most was held in the highest honour. It was chiefly to stop their head-hunting expeditions into British territory that in 1866 the Garo Hills were annexed. The expenditure is still about double the revenue.

The Garos, like other aboriginal tribes, believe in the existence of witches and imps of all kinds. They have the curious idea that certain persons are capable of leaving their human frames, and taking up their abode in the body of a tiger or other animal. At their funerals, all men, women, and children get drunk.

THE KHASIS.

The Khasis inhabit the hills to the east of the Garos. Their country is remarkable as containing Cherrapunji. with the greatest known rainfall in the world. The hills

EUROPEAN CROMLECH.

contain fine limestone, which is exported in large quantities to Calcutta.

In 1881 Khasi was spoken by about 110,000. The language is monosyllabic, and, so far as yet known, peculiar. The following is a specimen :—

> Naba kumta U Blei u la ſeit ia ka pyrthei, katba u la aití-noh ia la U Khún ia u ba-la-khamarwei, ba uei-uei-ruh u bangeit ha u, u'n 'nu'm jot shub, hinrei u'n ioh ka jingim b'ymjiukut.

The Khasis bury the ashes of their dead under four upright stones, covered over by a fifth stone on the top. The picture on the previous page represents stones of this kind used in ancient Europe, but the bodies were sometimes enclosed, not the ashes. They are called cromlechs.

The Khasis were formerly rude like the Garos. Missionaries have gone among them, reduced their language to writing, printed books, and opened schools. In 1881 the number of Khasi Christians was 2,763, and the schools contained 2,242 pupils.

LUSHAIS OR KUKIS.

The Lushais, or Kukis, are hill tribes to the east of Chittagong and south of Cachar. They are under hereditary chiefs, the number of whose followers depends upon the success which attends their border forays. The chief exercises absolute power in the village; he has a large number of slaves, and his free subjects contribute labour. Like other hill tribes, they make clearings in the forest and plant rice; but their main occupation is hunting and fighting. The men are well made and very strong, but of a sulky and forbidding cast of countenance.

Men, women, and children, from the age at which they can hold a pipe, smoke incessantly. Tobacco water is carried about in small gourds, and sipped from occasionally, being kept for a short time in the mouth before it is spat out. This tobacco water is looked upon as a great luxury, and when a Lushai meets a friend he offers it to him as a mark of courtesy. The men wear necklaces of beads. A large tiger's tooth, mounted in silver, and suspended round the neck by a thread, is much prized as a charm.

From the earliest times the Lushais have been notorious for their bloody raids into British territory, partly for the sake of plunder, partly to obtain human heads for use at their funeral ceremonies. In every village there is a rudely formed figure of wood, of human shape, representing their god. When the Lushais return successful after one of their expeditions, the heads of the slain are placed before this image. Each warrior has his own particular pile of heads ; and according to the number his character is established in the tribe. These piles are sacred ; no man dares take away any of the heads to add to his own.

In 1860, the Lushais made a raid into the district of Tipperah, in which 186 Bengali villagers were massacred, and 100 carried away into captivity. In 1871 they made attacks on villages in Cachar, Sylhet, and Tipperah. A tea planter was killed, and his daughter was carried off. This led to expeditions into the country, when 15 chiefs tendered their submission, and the planter's daughter and upwards of 100 Bengalis were liberated from captivity.

In 1890 the Lushais again gave trouble. Two expeditions were sent, one from Chittagong, the other from Burma, which met in the middle of the country. A fort was established, and means taken to open up the country by roads. The people will gradually become civilised.

LEPCHAS.

The Lepchas are a small tribe, inhabiting Sikkim, a mountainous district in the Himalayas, due north of Calcutta. Darjeeling, in the south, is reached by rail from Calcutta, and is a health resort during the hot season.

The Lepcha features are Mongolian, or somewhat like the Chinese. The stature is short, the face broad and flat, the eye oblique, chin beardless, the skin yellowish. The legs and arms are strong. In disposition the Lepcha is timid and peaceful.

The chief article in a Lepcha dress is a cotton cloak, striped with blue and worked with white and red, which is loosely thrown round the body so as to leave the arms free. In cold weather an upper garment, with loose sleeves, is added. The hat, when worn, is made of leaves spread out between two thin plates of bamboo extravagantly broad, and with a hemispherical crown.

A MAHARANI OF SIKKIM.

The ornaments are chiefly of Tibetan make, some having in them little idols, charms, copies of prayers, bones, hairs, and nail-parings of their priests, called lamas. The hair, an object of pride and care, in the dressing of which a female will assist a male, is collected into a large tail—simple or plaited, flat or round. The women wear two tails. Besides the skirt and petticoat, they wear a small sleeveless woollen cloak, covered with crosses, and fastened by a girdle of silver. A coronet of scarlet cloth adorns the head. The common dress is of tusser silk.

LEPCHA WATER-CARRIER.

The Lepchas drink out of neat little wooden cups. They make a kind of beer from grain.

The priests are their medicine men, the drivers out of evil spirits, the directors of feasts, ceremonies, and sacrifices. These are to the evil rather than the good spirits. "Why should we sacrifice to *them*? They do us no harm. The evil spirits, who dwell in every rock, grove, and mountain, are constantly at mischief, and to them we must pray, for it is they who hurt us."

Omens are sought from the entrails of fowls. Among their charms are the dog-tooth of a leopard, an ornamented brass bead, a piece of ginger, the hard seeds of some tree, sometimes all strung on a thread, and placed round the neck of a child to protect it from harm.

The Lepchas are skilful in kindling a light by means of two pieces of wood.

Christian missions were commenced among the Lepchas in 1870. Some books have been printed in their language, and a number have become Christians.

SUNWAR WOMAN.

THE NEPALESE.

NEPAL is an independent State on the Himalayas, between Tibet and British territory. It is very mountainous, and contains Mount Everest, 29,002 feet in height, the loftiest known peak in the world.

The country is inhabited by a variety of races. The aboriginal inhabitants appear to be of Tartar or Chinese origin, bearing no resemblance to the Hindus either in features, religion or manners. One of them, the Sunwar, represented on the previous page is found in the Western Hills.

The Gurkhas are the ruling race in Nepal. They are said to have emigrated from Tirhut in the 14th century A.D. Their language resembles Hindi; but about one-fifth of the words have been adopted from Tibetan, &c.

GURKHAS.

The Gurkhas are small men, not remarkable for their beauty. They are brave soldiers and hunters. They carry with them a large heavy knife. It is carved on both the hilt and blade, and can be used equally well for stabbing and cutting. The Gurkhas will fearlessly await the spring of a tiger, when, agile as monkeys, they will leap aside, at the same moment adroitly drawing the knife across the tiger's throat. By the combined force with which the blow was struck, and the impetus of the animal itself, in a flood of blood, the tyrant of the Indian jungle lies dead at the Gurkha's feet. Generally the death of the tiger is not accomplished by one blow, but by several delivered at each spring of the infuriated beast.

The Gurkhas worship chiefly the goddess Kali. It is the same with some other hill tribes. In Kangra, on the Himalayas, human sacrifices were offered to Kali up to the time that it came under the British. An old cedar tree was cut down only a few years ago to which a girl was offered annually, the families of the village taking it in turn to supply the victim. When the Viceroy opened the Sirhind Canal in 1882, the people of the lower hills believed that 200 of the prisoners who had been employed on the works were released on condition of their furnishing a similar number of girls to be sacrificed at the inaugural ceremony, and lit fires and beat drums and sat up for several nights in order to keep off any who might be prowling about in search of female children.

There are a few regiments of Gurkhas in the British Indian army.

TIBETANS.

Tibet is under China; but as there are upwards of 20,000 Tibetans in British India, some account will be given of them and their country.

Tibet lies to the north of India, with the Himalayas in the south and the Kuen-lun chain in the north. It is the highest tableland in the world, its mean height above the sea being nearly three miles. It contains several lakes, and the sources of the Indus, Sutlej, and Brahmaputra. The cold in winter is very severe. Some grain is raised in the valleys; but the people are chiefly pastoral. Sheep, goats, and the *yak*, a kind of buffalo, are the principal domestic quadrupeds. The sheep are of the broad-tailed species, and are employed as beasts of burden. The goats are covered with fine hair which is largely exported.

TIBETAN LAMA.

The Tibetans belong to the Mongolian race. They are strong and hardy. Their language is written syllabically, each syllable being separated by a wedge-like sign.

The Tibetans are chiefly remarkable for their religion, a form of Buddhism, mixed up with demon worship and magic. The head of the religion, called the Grand Lama, is supposed to be an incarnation of the coming Buddha. Besides him, there are others supposed to be avatars of Buddhist sages. There are a great many inferior priests. Their sacred books, called the Tanjur, consist of 225 volumes.

SAINT WAVING DORJE.

When the Grand Lama dies, or, as it is thought, when his soul passes into another body, the names of all the male children born at the time have to be sent to Lhassa, the capital. Three children are selected; their names are written and placed in a golden urn. The child whose name is drawn out is proclaimed Grand Lama. He is carried through the city with great pomp, and placed in the golden temple which he never leaves. The Grand Lama often dies young, supposed to be secretly murdered by those who wish to rule in his name.

PRIEST AND PRAYING CYLINDER.

The priests wear a yellow or red dress. It should be made out of rags; but the cold climate requires warm clothing. The law is supposed to be obeyed by putting a patch or two at the corner.

Every priest has an instrument made of metal, called a *dorje*, (Sanskrit, *vajra*), a thunderbolt. It is held between the fingers and thumb, and waved backwards and forwards to drive away evil spirits. In the picture on page 38 one of the Buddhist saints is represented as waving the dorje.

A priest has also a bell. It is rung to call the attention of the beings who are worshipped.

Great importance is attached to a prayer, called the six-syllabled sentence, *Om mani padme Hum*, "Om, the Jewel in the Lotus, Hum." Every Tibetan believes this to be a cure for all evil, a compendium of all knowledge, a summary of all religion. It is supposed that the oftener this formula is repeated, the shorter will be a person's course of transmigration. These six syllables are murmured morning, noon, and night, by every man, woman, and child in Tibet.

The words are written or printed on rolls and inscribed in cylinders, to turn round, which is thought to have the same efficacy as to have them repeated. If the words are printed a million times, to turn round the cylinder once is equal to repeating them a million times! There are little prayer wheels, which the more devout carry with them, turning them round with the hand or a string. There are large barrel-like cylinders containing the words written lakhs of times. The picture on page 39 represents one of these which a priest is turning with a string, while reading his sacred books.

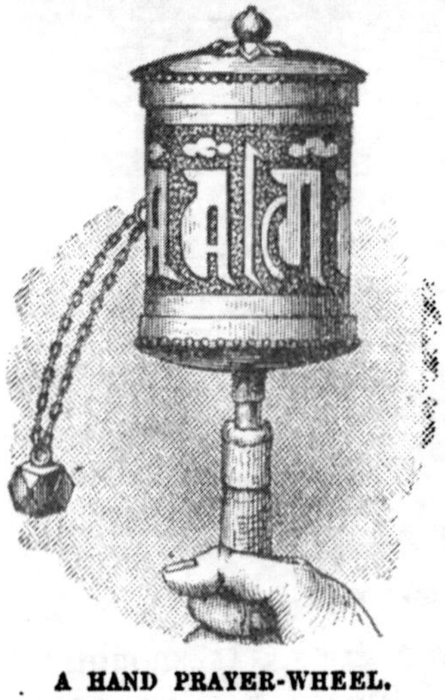

A HAND PRAYER-WHEEL.

A favourite plan is to set a prayer wheel where it will be turned day and night by a stream of running water. Thus the Tibetan, asleep or awake, supposes that he is laying up a stock of merit. In some cases, there are large wheels supplying merit for a whole village.

Flags are also erected on which the six holy syllables are embroidered. Whenever they are blown by the wind, it counts as a repetition.

Europeans are forbidden to enter Tibet. Some missionaries from Germany have been waiting for years at Kyelang, on the borders, where there are some Tibetans. The Bible has been partly translated into Tibetan, other books have been written, and a few Tibetans have become Christians.

URIYAS OR ORIYAS.

The Uriyas, about seven millions in number, are chiefly found in Orissa, to the south-west of Bengal. The province is about the size of Oudh. The name is derived from Odradesa, the country of the Odras. In ancient times it was called Utkala. It was conquered by the Mahrattas, from whom it was taken by the British in 1803.

The shores are low, marshy, and subject to inundations of the sea. Farther inland, there are fertile undulating tracts; but the greater part of the interior consists of rugged hills, covered with jungle and infested by wild beasts.

The Uriya language is very like Bengali. It is the only one of the North Indian characters which has adopted the curved form of the upper strokes. This was necessary from writing on palm leaves with an iron pen; straight lines would have cut the leaf. Some of the letters are very like each other.

ORIYA, or Uriya. (*Orissa.*)

ଯେହେତୁ ତାହାଙ୍କଠାରେ ପ୍ରତ୍ୟେକ ଜଣ ବିଶ୍ୱାସକାରୀ ଯେମନ୍ତ
ନଷ୍ଟ ନ ହୋଇ ଅନନ୍ତ ପରମାୟୁ ପାଇବ ଏଥିପାଁଇ ଈଶ୍ୱର ଜଗତକୁ
ଏତେ ପ୍ରେମ କଲେ ଯେ ସେ ଆପଣା ଅଦ୍ୱିତୀୟ ପୁତ୍ରକୁ ଦେଲେ

Dr. Cust says that Uriya has a literature, the earliest monuments of which date back three hundred years.

Mr. Beverley, in 1872, thus described the Uriyas :—

"The Ooriyas are even more timid than the Bengalis. Conservative to a degree, they are wanting in enterprise, contented to follow the practices of their forefathers, and evincing a thorough dislike of all modern improvements. The same characteristic makes them the most bigoted and priest-ridden people in India."

The Province has been greatly neglected. In some inland parts, a cart is as great a novelty as a balloon elsewhere. Hitherto it has had no railroads, and the ordinary roads are very inferior. Hence Orissa suffered terribly during famines. There is now canal communication with Calcutta, and the East Coast Railway passes through the Province. Education is improving. In British Orissa one boy, out of every three of school-going age, is at school. There is a College at Cuttack. In 1901, the number of Christians in the Province was over 6,000.

JAGANNATH.

Orissa is especially noted for the worship of Jagannath. For several hundred years the religion was Buddhism. One of Buddha's supposed teeth was said to have been brought to Puri, 543 B.C. A new dynasty, which arose about 474 A.D., re-established Brahmanism.

The following is one legend with regard to the origin of the image of Jagannath at Puri. When Krishna was shot, his bones were left lying under the tree till some pious person placed them in a box. Indradhumma, a king, was directed to form an image, and place in it these bones. The king prayed to Visvakarma to assist him in making the image. The architect of the gods promised to do so on condition that he was not disturbed. Though the king consented, after fifteen days he tried to see Visvakarma at work, but there was only an ugly image, without hands or feet. By the image there is generally one of Balarama, Krishna's brother, and his sister Subhadra.

The temple is called *Swarga Dwara*, the gate of heaven. A tract sold at the door states that "Even Siva is unable to comprehend its glory; how feeble then the efforts of mortal men!" Lascivious sculptures disfigure its walls, indecent ceremonies disgrace its ritual, and dancing girls take part in its worship.

There are large numbers of men, called *Pandas*, pilgrim-hunters, who go about the country in all directions to entice people to visit Puri. They represent that all sorts of advantages will result from this meritorious act. The ground around Puri is said to be all strewn with gold, although, on account of the wickedness of the Kali-yug, it appears to be common dust. Many of the pilgrims are women, who sometimes follow these pilgrim-hunters against the consent of their male relatives. Numbers die by the way. Skeletons lie scattered along the sides of the roads on the principal routes.

Sir W. W. Hunter says: "Disease and death make havoc of the pilgrims. During their stay in Puri they are badly lodged and miserably fed." Pilgrims are told that it is sinful for them to cook themselves. They must buy the food, *mahaprasad*, which has been presented to Jagannath. The price is dear, the cooking bad, and often it is so old as to be putrid. It is considered too sacred for the least fragment to be thrown away. Hence it is consumed by some one or other, whatever its state of putrefaction, to the very last morsel. It is dangerous even to a man of robust health, and deadly to way-worn pilgrims, many of whom reach Puri with some form or other of bowel complaint.

THE JUANGS.

The Juangs, in the Hill districts of Orissa, are one of the most degraded tribes in India, though they claim to be the first produced of the human race. They are probably a remnant of one of the forest tribes that originally peopled India, whose stone implements are found in different parts of the country.

They had, till lately, no knowledge of iron. They neither spin nor weave, nor have the least knowledge of pottery. The women used not to wear a particle of clothing, but bunches of leaves before and behind, hanging to a girdle of beads. They were afraid to wear clothes, believing that if they did they would be devoured by tigers.

In 1871 an English officer called together the clan, and after a speech handed out strips of cotton cloth for the women to put on. They then passed in single file to the number of 1,900, making obeisance. Finally they gathered the bunches of leaves together which had formed their sole clothing into a great heap and set fire to it. It is reported, however, that a number of the Juang women, their original garments wearing out and finding that they were not to be renewed gratuitously, have again lapsed into their leafy attire. The women tattoo their faces with three strokes on the forehead just over the nose, and three on each of the temples.

The Juangs have curious dances. In the bear dance they imitate the bear. The pigeon dance, pig and tortoise dance, cock and hen dance, are others of a similar kind. In the vulture dance one man is made to represent a dead body. The girls in approaching him imitate the hopping, sidling advance of the bird of prey, and using their hands as beaks, nip and pinch the supposed corpse, so that occasionally he forgets his character and yells with pain. This affords great amusement.

The Juangs have no belief in witchcraft. So far as known, their language has no words for 'God,' 'heaven,' 'hell.' They offer fowls to the sun when in distress, and to the earth to give them its fruits in due season.

THE KHONDS.

The Khonds, or Kandhs, are found in the south-east of Orissa and the adjoining districts of the Central Provinces and Madras Presidency. The name denotes hill men. They are estimated to number about 430,000.

The Khonds belong to the Dravidian race, and have occupied the same part of the country for 1,500 years. Their language, the Khond or Ku, in some respects, resembles Tamil and Kanarese closer than its nearer neighbour the Telugu. Thus, he (remote) is *avánu* in Khond, *avan* in Tamil, *avanu* in Kanarese, and *vádu* in Telugu.

The Khond family is strictly ruled by the father. The grown-up sons have no property during his life, but live in his house with their wives and children, and all share the common meal prepared by the grandmother.

Murders were punished by blood-revenge, the kinsmen within a certain degree being one and all bound to kill the slayer, unless appeased by a payment of grain or cattle. The man who accidentally or wrongfully wounded another had to maintain the sufferer until he recovered from his hurt. A stolen article must be returned or its equivalent paid; but the Khond twice convicted of theft was driven forth from his tribe, the greatest punishment known to the race. Disputes were settled by combat, or by the ordeal of boiling oil or heated iron, or by taking a solemn oath on an ant-hill, or on a tiger's claw, or a lizard's skin. The tribe was summoned to war by an arrow borne by swift messengers from glen to glen. The Khond adorned himself for war as for a feast. The most approved form was to go on fighting day after day until one party or the other was exterminated.

An eye-witness has described a conflict which lasted for three days. The women and old men past bearing arms stood close by the combatants during the battle, handing them pots of water and cooked food, with much good advice as to the conduct of the fight. When the first man fell, all rushed to dip their axes in his blood, and hacked his body to pieces; while the man who slew his enemy without getting a wound himself hewed off the right arm from the corpse, and ran with it to the priest among the non-combatants in the rear, as an offering to the God of War. Before evening a great heap of right arms had thus accumulated in each rear—one side having lost 60 men and the other 30, besides at least as many more mortally wounded as the result of the first day's fight. The Khond never claims victory as the reward of his personal valour, but always ascribes it to the favour of his god.

The Khonds have many deities, race-gods, tribe-gods, family-gods, and a multitude of malignant spirits and demons. But their great divinity is the Earth-goddess, upon whom the fertility of their fields was supposed to depend. Twice each year, at sowing time and harvest, before or after a battle, and in all seasons of special calamity, the Earth-goddess required a human sacrifice.

Children were kidnapped from the plains. The victim, on being brought to the village, was welcomed at every threshold, daintily fed, and kindly treated, till the fatal day arrived. He was then tied to a post. The priest said, "We have bought you with a price, and no sin rests on us." To prevent his offering any resistance, his arms and legs were broken with a hatchet. The priest first cut off a portion of the flesh from the body and offered it to the Earth-goddess. All the people then cut the flesh from the bones and buried it in their fields to make them fertile.

In 1835 the Khonds passed under British rule. Special officers were appointed to suppress human sacrifices, and many children, intended as victims, were rescued, and either returned to their parents or sent to schools. The Khonds now allow that their crops grow as well without as with human sacrifices.

Among the Khonds in Bastar small-pox is common, and numerous temples are dedicated to Mata Devi. The patient,

HUMAN SACRIFICE AMONG THE KHONDS.

into whose body the goddess is deemed to have entered, is treated with scrupulous regard. As soon as the disease shows itself, his feet are washed with cow's milk, and carefully wiped upon the head of his nearest relative. Mata Devi is then prayed to take under her special protection the family whom she has honoured with a visit; the patient is placed upon a bed of fresh rice-straw, with a screen around him; his friends constantly repair to the temple of Mata Devi and anoint her image with ground sandal-wood and water, with which they then sprinkle the house where the patient lies and sign his forehead. His diet consists of fruit and cooling food and drink; but no medicines are administered. Though vaccination is unknown, inoculation is practised to some extent.

Some Khonds in the south, called Kois, will be noticed separately.

THE GONDS.

In old maps of India a large territory was marked *Gondawana*, which is now included in the Central Provinces. The Gonds are found in different parts between the Vindhya Mountains and the Godavari, and from the country of the Khonds as far as Khandesh and Malwa. At the last Census the number returned as speaking Gondi was upwards of a million.

At one time the Gonds and Khonds were supposed to be the same; but their languages are very different. Gondi is remarkable for its elaborate conjugational system. While the Tamil verb has only three tenses, Gondi has six.

The history of the Gonds is very imperfectly known. They say that they had several lines of kings. There are inscriptions claiming that some of their princes, by their beneficence, made earth better than heaven, how the world trembled at the march of their elephants, and how the sea was swollen by the tears of queens widowed by their conquests! At present they are in a low state of civilization.

The Gonds are about the middle size. They have the black skin, flat nose, and thick lips which proclaim them of other than Aryan blood. Nearly all dress in the same way. For both sexes a cloth wound about the waist constitutes the chief article of attire. Necklaces of beads, ear-rings of brass and iron, brass bracelets, and girdles of twisted cords, find favour in the eyes of young men and women.

They seldom wear any covering on the head. Women often wear false hair. In one of their hymns, the god blames the Gonds for not bathing for six months together. Their dirtiness and the tattoo marks on their faces, arms, and thighs, repel Europeans. They are more truthful than the Hindus, but arrant thieves. All are fond of music and dancing. Sometimes they form a ring by joining hands and advance a step towards the centre, and again retire while circling round and round. When wearied with dancing, they sing. A man steps out of the crowd and sings a verse; a woman rejoins, and the pair chant in alternate strains, for the most part rallying each other on personal defects. All are addicted to drinking.

The Gonds are divided into several religious sects, worshipping different gods. In some parts Thakur Deo is held in great reverence. He is the household god, presiding over the homestead and the farmyard; and, being omnipresent, requires no image to represent him. Cholera and small-pox are worshipped under the names of Mari and Mata Devi. To appease the wrath of these divinities, they offer sacrifices; and cleaning their villages they place the sweepings on a road or track, in the hope that some traveller will be infected, and so convey the disease to another village. In addition to his gods, the Gond peoples the forests with spirits of all kinds, most of them able and only too willing to inflict evil upon him. To propitiate them he sets up a bamboo with a piece of rag tied to the end, or the like. There the spirit takes up his abode, and there, at each festival in the family, the spirit has his share of the feast.

When a Gond falls victim to a tiger, a priest is called to lay the spirit of the dead, and to charm away the additional power which the tiger has derived from his prey. The priest goes through certain movements, representing the tiger in its fatal spring; and, lastly, takes up with his teeth a mouthful of the blood-stained earth.

The Gonds, like many other aboriginal tribes, have a strong belief in witchcraft. A man's wife or his child gets sick. Instead of ascribing it to bad food or some such cause, it is put down to witchcraft, and the supposed witch is beaten to death.

In some parts there are temples to Kali in which human sacrifices were offered. The victim was taken to the temple after sunset, and shut up within it. In the morning he was found dead, the great goddess having come by night and sucked his blood. Some one was hid in the temple to kill the victim. There is a famous temple of Kali in the Native State of Bastar. About sixty years ago it is said that upwards of 25 full-grown men were immolated on a single occasion by a Raja of Bastar.

There are a few Christian Missionaries labouring among the Gonds, and portions of the Bible have been translated into their language.

THE SANTALS.

The Santals are scattered over a curved strip of country, about 350 miles in length, extending from the Ganges to the river Baitarani. In the western jungles they are the only population, but generally they are mixed with the Hindus of the plains. They number about 11 lakhs.

The Santals belong to the Kolarian race, who are supposed to have entered India from the north-east. The Santal is more squarely built than the Hindu, with a forehead not so high, but rounder and broader; the lips are a little thicker than those of the Aryan; the hair is straight, coarse and black. The cast of countenance somewhat resembles the negro type.

The language, which is distinct from the Northern and Southern families, is noted for its numerous inflections. Its verb system has five voices, five moods, twenty-three tenses, three numbers, and four cases. The language is unwritten, and is now rendered in Roman and Bengali characters.

> **Nonká báre ápe hon h[illegible]ko samángre marsál gnel ochoitápe jemon unko hon [illegible]: bugi kámi gnelkáte áperen sermàren ja:námi: ko sarhaue.**—(*Matt.* v. 16.)

SANTAL IDOL.

The Santals do not care for permanently locating themselves; but their huts, with carefully formed mud walls and gaily painted with stripes of red, white, and black, are neat and clean.

The Santals dress better than most of the tribes around them. The women wear ample *saris*, not less than six yards in length, with a gay red border. Their arms, ankles, and throats are laden with heavy brass ornaments. Their average weight may be estimated at six seers, but some weigh as much as seventeen seers.

There is a national antagonism between the Santals and Hindus. The Santals are not over-particular about food, but nothing will induce them to eat rice cooked by a Hindu —even by a Brahman. This was not known to Government during the famine of 1866. The cooks were all Brahmans, but the Santals kept aloof, and died rather than eat from hands so hateful to them. They have no tradition to account for this bitter feeling.

The national instrument of music is the flute, made of bamboo, not less than one inch in diameter and about two feet in length: its tones are deep and rich. The Santals say that the faculty of playing the flute and a general knowledge of singing and dancing were imparted to them by their first parents. It was also by their first parents, they say, that they were taught to prepare rice-beer, and they therefore consider that there can be no great harm in freely indulging in it.

There is always an open space in a village for dancing. To this the young men frequently resort after the evening meal. The sound of their flutes and drums soon attract the maidens, who smooth their long hair, and adding to it a flower or two, blithely join them.

The Santals have every year a great hunting festival in which thousands take part. It takes place in the hot season, when the beasts have least cover to conceal themselves in. They form a line of beaters several miles in length, each man armed with a bow and arrows and a battle-axe, and accompanied by dogs. When wild animals are thus driven together, birds are shot with arrows; deer, pigs, hares, &c., are killed; but tigers and bears on these occasions are generally avoided.

The dead are burned. The body is borne away on a cot

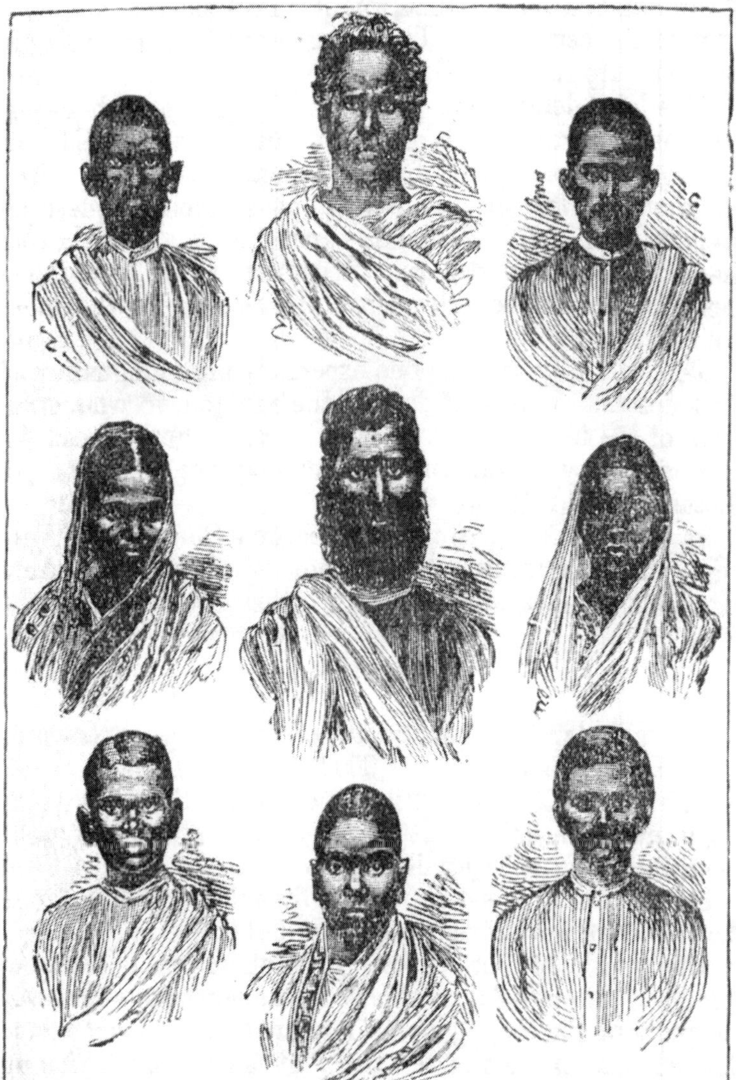

SANTAL CHRISTIANS.

by kinsmen, and when it reaches a cross road, some parched rice and cotton seeds are scattered about as a charm against the malignant spirits that might throw obstacles in the way of the ceremony. The bones saved from the pile are thrown into the river Damodar.

The local demons are propitiated by sacrifice when disease or misfortune visits a family. In the eastern districts the tiger is worshipped, but in Ramgarh only those who have suffered loss through that animal's ferocity condescend to adore him. If a Santal is carried off by a tiger, the head of the family deems it necessary to propitiate the tiger *bhút*. To be sworn on a tiger's skin, is the most solemn of oaths.

The Santal gods, with one exception, are malignant and destructive. The chief deity is the sun-god, to whom the head of the family about every third year offers a goat for the prosperity of children that they may not be cut off by disease or fall into sin.

Several thousand Santals have become Christians. Portions of the Scriptures have been translated into their language, besides educational and other books.

ORAONS.

The table-land of Chota (more correctly Chutia) Nagpore is a beautiful region about 2,000 feet above the level of the sea, about 14,000 square miles in extent, with rivers flowing in every direction. It is inhabited by different tribes, the principal of which will be noticed.

The Oraons are best known as Dhangars, hill men, from the apparent derivative *dhang*, hill; but the term is applied to the youth of both sexes, in highland and lowland villages. Though found chiefly in the northern and western parts of Chota Nagpore, there are scattered offshoots. Colonel Dalton estimates them at about six lakhs in number. They are an industrious race, known far and wide as day labourers.

The language is Dravidian, but it has been considerably influenced by Aryan contact. The tradition is that the tribe gradually emigrated from Western India.

Their huts are badly constructed and huddled together. Groups of houses are built in rows of three or four facing each other, and forming a small enclosed court, seldom properly drained or cleared. In their huts the human beings and cattle have common tenancy. The pigs alone have buildings appropriated to their own use.

The walls are of mud, but when constructed of red laterite soil they are as durable as if built of brick. The worst of this method of building is that holes are dug to supply the material, which are, ever afterwards, receptacles of filth and hot-beds of fever.

Very few villages are now found tenanted only by Oraons. The majority have been assigned to middlemen whose more pretentious tiled dwellings, with their upper stories, look down on the low thatched gable-ended huts of the aborigines.

The headman is the functionary to whom the proprietor of the village looks for its secular administration. He may be removed if he fail to give satisfaction.

A priest there must be; an Oraon community cannot get on without one. The office does not go from father to son. The latter may be ignorant and disqualified; he may be a Christian. When vacated it is filled by divination. The fate of the village is in the priest's hands; in their own phraseology, it is said that "he makes its affairs." He is also master of the revels which are for the most part connected with religious rites. The doctrine of the Oraons is that man best pleases the gods, when he makes himself merry. Thus acts of worship and propitiatory sacrifices are always associated with feasting, drinking, dancing, and love-making.

In all the older Oraon villages there is a house in which all the bachelors of the village must, when not absent from it, sleep under penalty of a fine.

Immediately in front of the sleeping hall is the dancing arena, about 40 feet in diameter, with a stone or post marking its centre. It is surrounded by seats for tired dancers or non-dancing spectators, and shaded by fine old tamarind trees. During the festive seasons of the year, dancing commences shortly after dark every night, and if the supply of liquor holds out, is often kept up till sunrise. On some occasions the ground is laid down with red earth, which pulverises under the many twinkling feet and rises in a lurid cloud about the dancers till the garments, the dusky skins, and the black hair of the performers become all of a brick dust hue.

The Oraon women are all tattooed in childhood with three marks on the brow and two on each temple. The young men burn marks on the fore-arm. This is part of the discipline boys have to go through to make them hardy and manly. Girls, when adults or nearly so, have themselves further tattooed on the arms and back.

The Oraons acknowledge a Supreme God who is manifest in the sun. He is beneficent, but does not interfere if the spirit of evil once fastens upon us. It is of no use to pray to Him; He is therefore neglected, whilst malignant spirits are adored.

Some Oraons have become Christians, partly because God will protect them, and that witches and *bhuts* will have no power over them.

Oraons suppose that men who are killed by tigers become tigers; but for other people death is annihilation. They tremblingly wander in a world of ghosts. Every rock, road, river and grave is haunted. They believe that women who die in childbirth become ghosts, and such ghosts are frequently met, hovering about the tombstones, always clad in robes of white, their faces fair and lovely, but with backs black as charcoal, and inverted feet; that is, they walk with their heels in front. They lay hold of passers-by and wrestle with them and tickle them, and he is lucky indeed who, thus caught, escapes without permanent injuries.

KOLS.

This name is sometimes applied to all the Kolarian tribes; but it is used by Europeans chiefly to denote the Munda

Kols, the Larka (fighting) Kols or Hos, and the Bhumiji Kols. The name is considered disrespectful, and is not used by the tribes themselves.

According to tradition, the Kols were once a powerful race in Behar, the ancient Magadha. Numerous forts and ruins are ascribed to them. At present they are found chiefly in the mountainous districts and table-lands of Chota Nagpore. They are subdivided into clans, each called after an animal, plant or tree. The rule is that a member of a particular clan, such as the snakes, tortoises, or mango trees, must not marry women of the group.

Each Mundari village has a chief, called a *múnda*, 'a head,' in Sanskrit, and as a village often consisted of one family, it became a name for the whole tribe.

Some of the women wear very heavy bracelets, armlets, and anklets of bell metal. It is a singular sight to see the young women at a market subjecting themselves to the torture of being fitted with a pair of these anklets. They are made so that they can just, with great violence, be forced on. The operation is performed by the manufacturers, who put moistened leather on the heel and instep to prevent excoriation. The girl clinging to and resting on one of her companions cries bitterly at the violence inflicted on her, and the operation is a long one; but when it is over, she admires her decorated foot and instep and smiles through her tears.

The Ho women have adopted as their distinctive mark an arrow, which they regard as their national emblem. A Ho unable to write, if asked to attach his mark or sign manual to a document, does so by making a rude representation of an arrow.

The Kols breed ducks and geese, and they have sheep and goats for food, but it is generally for the purpose of propitiatory sacrifices that they are slaughtered and eaten. Bullocks and buffaloes are also reared. The Kols, like most of the Indo-Chinese races, make no use of the milk.

The Kols generally eat beef, mutton, fowls, and fish; but, unlike the Santals and Oraons, they do not approve of the flesh of bears, monkeys, snakes and mice. They will take from Europeans cakes and bread, but not cooked rice. In regard to cooked rice they are very particular. They will leave off eating, if a man's shadow passes across their food.

An equal division of property among the sons is the prevailing custom of inheritance; but they live together as an undivided family until the youngest attains his majority, when the division is made. The sisters are regarded as live-stock and are allotted to the brothers like cattle. The price of a wife is usually six head of cattle. If there are three brothers and one sister, each gets two head of cattle on the marriage of the latter. Owing to the high prices placed on daughters by their fathers, a large number of adult unmarried girls may be seen in every considerable village. The girls complain that the young men "do not propose."

After the birth of a child, both father and mother are considered unclean for eight days, during which period the other members of the family are sent out of the house, and the husband has to cook for his wife. In a case of difficult labour, some evil spirit is supposed to be at work, and after divination to ascertain his name, a sacrifice is made to appease him At the expiration of the eight days, the banished members of the family return, friends are invited to a feast, and the child is ceremoniously named. The name of the grandfather is usually given to the first born son, but not without taking an omen to ascertain if it will prove fortunate. As the name is mentioned a grain of pulse is thrown into a vessel with water; the name is adopted if it floats, rejected if it sinks.

Like many other wild tribes, the Kols are very fond of dancing. They breed fowls from their great love of cock-fighting. At all market places on market days and at other places on fixed days, they have great meetings for this amusement. The cocks are armed with cruel steel spurs, and the combat is always to the death, the winning cock gaining for his master the corpse of his foe.

The sun is worshipped as the supreme divinity. He is said to have married the moon, but she deceived him on

KOL DANCE.

one occasion and he cut her in two; but repenting of his anger, he allows her at times to shine forth in full beauty. The stars are her daughters.

The next in order among the gods is the mountain god. He is supposed to bring rain, and therefore receives special attention. Every third year, in most places, buffaloes are sacrificed in his honour, and fowls and goats every year. He is also invoked in sickness. Every village has in its vicinity a grove for the local gods. They are held responsible for the crops, and are especially honoured at all the great agricultural festivals. Then follow the spirits that preside over tanks and wells. The remaining spirits are the ancestral shades who are supposed to hover about, doing good or evil to their descendants. A small portion of the food prepared in every house is daily set apart for them.

All disease in men or animals is attributed to one of two causes—the wrath of some evil spirit who has to be appeased, or to the spell of some witch or sorcerer who should be destroyed or driven out of the land. In the latter a witch-finder is employed to divine who has cast the spell, and various modes of divination are resorted to. In former times the person denounced and all his family were put to death in the belief that witches breed witches.

The ghost of a Ho likes to have his grave all to himself. It is indicated by a massive stone from five to fifteen feet in height.* Collections of them mark the site of every Ho or Mundari village.

In 1901 there were 62,000 Christians among the Kols and other tribes in Chota Nagpore. The New Testament has been printed in Mundari.

Mundari, like the Santal, belongs to the Kolarian family. The language was unwritten. The Nagri character is employed in writing it.

* See illustration, page 3.

INDIAN GYPSIES.

Gipsy, or Gypsy, is the name given to a wandering race, some of them scattered over Europe. It means *Egyptian*, because they were supposed to come from Egypt. Their language, however, containing many Hindi words, shows that they are of Indian origin. Some Gipsy tribes are still found in India. Two of them are thus described by *The Pioneer* :—

"The Bengal Gypsies call themselves in their own jargon, *Kathwais* or *Bhatus*, but in order to evade suspicion and troublesome inquiries as to antecedents, they assume the suffix Ahir, Rowasu, Kanjhar, or Kushmiri. A widely-spread tradition current among them identifies them with the Sansias, a nomad race of Rajputana, of which we shall have occasion to say something more presently. In the matter of religion Nats (dancers) are professed Hindus. Like the Thugs, they worship Kali, the robbers' patron deity, and when about to undertake a *coup* they propitiate her with sacrifices of goats and buffaloes. They bury the bodies of their dead children, but cremate adults, and carry the bones of chiefs to Hurdwar to mingle them with the sacred Ganges. They observe the Hindu ceremony called *sasthi*, which takes place six days after the naming of a new-born male infant. The women bore their noses; the men their ears, making the piercing of the lobe an occasion for distributing sweetmeats in honour of their *gurus*. The latter are called Dhula and Maukhan, and according to a popular story, they flourished at some unknown period in Jodhpur or Bikanir. Like the uneducated of all countries Nats mingle many gross superstitions with religious forms. Saturday and Thursday are deemed highly inauspicious for business of any kind. If a Nat passes a snake on the left, hears a man sneezing behind him, or meets one who is lame, he postpones any undertaking which he may be meditating. Equally characteristic of a primitive social development are the Nat marriage customs.

Marriageable girls are sold by their father to a suitor for a sum which must exceed Rs. 200. Polygamy is unknown, but the re-marriage of widows is permitted, and in certain cases insisted on. The young Natins are often strikingly beautiful with large, dark eyes set in a perfect oval; and contrary to the usual belief, those who belong to the wandering tribes are generally chaste. Every gang is governed by a leader who succeeds to the command by sheer force of character; and, though Nats are divided into seventeen castes many of which do not intermarry, every member of a gang owes implicit obedience to his chief whether above or below him in caste. Disputes are settled by a punchayet of adult males, who punish offences against the Gypsy code, by levying a fine termed *chauthi*. The community ostensibly live by begging; but like their race everywhere, they wage a ceaseless war against society. All are thieves by nature and education. Their tents, consisting of skins stretched over a rude bamboo framework, are pitched in one of the patches of waste land to be found near every village, and the adults wander from house to house, begging and offering charms and simple ornaments for sale. But a sharp look-out is kept for unconsidered trifles, and the valuable points of each homestead and its cattle-sheds are carefully noted. When the position has been sufficiently reconnoitered a *coup* takes place. Half a dozen ryots find themselves minus their best cattle, or the victims of a burglary, entry having been effected by means of long, sharp knives. The gang then make a forced march of fifty or sixty miles, generally separating to render pursuit and identification more difficult. Nats find it easy to dispose of their loot. Shopkeepers are to be found in every bazaar who will purchase jewellery and bazaar vessels without asking questions. Farmers relieve them of stolen cattle, at fair market prices, and goats speedily find their way into the sempiternal stewpot which includes such strange flesh as that of pigs, dogs and jackals. The proceeds of these *razzias* are equally divided among the adult members of the gang in fixed proportions. Like their

European brethren, Nats have a secret cant enabling them to recognise one another and convey warnings of danger. In their jargon, "Go away" is *Khishi jat;* "A bad omen," *Salai shogun;* "All right," *Kuchchi hui;* and "No danger," *Khaban chiarch.* The effect of these shibboleths pronounced in Nat hearing is magical. Nats pass the dry months in moving with more or less rapidity from place to place; and the rainy months in certain favoured villages of Dinagepur, Purnea, Maldah, Murshidabad and Monghyr. When hard pressed they make for Nepal territory; but there they may not tarry, for Goorkha justice is swifter and severer than the lame-footed article dealt out on British soil.

"The Indian Gypsies, as we have seen, claim relationship with the Bikanir Sansias. The latter are a nomad race, well-known throughout Rajputana, who allege that they separated three centuries ago from the Jat community. Their name is, according to tradition, derived from a common ancestor, named Satsi Mal, who enjoined on his descendants a life of mendicancy with no settled abode and the use of moveable thatched huts (*sharki*). The Sansias of Bikanir eat the remains of food from Hindu and Mahomedan tables, and are therefore regarded as unclean by the proud Rajputs. They, however, profess Hinduism and pay special reverence to a demi-god, named Ramdeo. Temples, many of them boasting a hoary antiquity, are to be found throughout Bikanir which are universally allowed to have been erected by Sansias. Though spurned by orthodox Hindus, who bathe if a Sansia's shadow falls on them, they are regarded as poor relations by Jats, and a voluntary tax for their support is levied in many villages of the clan. Sansias use asses for the transport of their moveable habitations, and spend the cool months in travelling throughout Rajputana, lying *perdu* during the fierce heat. They are inveterate beggars and pilferers, and marriage with them, as with the Gypsies, is a sale, the maiden fetching Rs. 60 or more. The Sansias for their part repudiate all connection with the Bengal Nats, but the coincidence between the customs of the two communities is too close to be accidental. Gypsy characteristics are unmistakeable, however far apart the *habitats* of their curious race."

A HINDUSTANI SYCE.

HINDUSTANIS.

HINDUSTAN, a Persian word meaning *The Country of the Hindus,* is sometimes loosely used by English writers to denote the whole of India. More correctly, it is the country between the Vindhya Mountains and the Himalayas, bounded on the West by the Panjab, and on the East by Assam. Hindustanis, in this little volume, include the nations using the Hindi and Hindustani languages. They chiefly inhabit Behar, west of Bengal, the North-West Provinces, Oudh, and parts of Central India. Their country contains a great part of the valley of the Ganges.

The climate is not so moist as that of Bengal. It is warm in the hot season, but the winter is cold and bracing. The rainfall is insufficient, as a rule, for rice; wheat and different kinds of millet are chiefly grown.

People.—On account of the climate and more nourishing food, the Hindustanis are taller and stronger than the Bengalis. They are also purer Aryans. Instead of the bare heads of the Bengalis, they wear good turbans to protect them either from heat or cold; and instead of thin garments they have thick jackets of two folds, well stuffed and quilted. Over the whole a warm quilt of two or three yards length is thrown, or shawls are worn. They usually wrap themselves up in the quilt when they go to sleep.

Language.—Hindi is spoken over an area of about 250,000 square miles, and is the vernacular of about 70 millions. There are numerous local variations; but it may be divided into Behari, or Eastern Hindi, and Western Hindi. Benares Hindi leans towards the Sanskrit; Agra Hindi towards the Persian. On the boundaries Hindi melts into the surrounding languages. Beames says, "On the banks of the Mahananda river both Bengali and Hindi are spoken, and both equally badly."

111. HINDI, or Hindui. (*N. India.*)

क्योंकि ईश्वरने जगतको ऐसा प्यार किया कि उसने अपना एकलौता पुत्र दिया कि जो कोई उसपर बिश्वास करे सो नाश न होय परन्तु अनन्त जीवन पावे।

Hindi is generally printed in the Nagri character. For quicker writing, a form called Kaithi is adopted. A still simpler form is used in commerce, called Sarafi or Mahajani.

HINDUSTANI or URDU is a mixed language. For a long time the Muhammadan conquerors of India spoke Persian, and the conquered, Hindi. By the soldiers and people talking to each other, a camp (Urdu) language was formed, containing a mixture of Hindi, Persian, and Arabic. It is usually written in the Persian character, and printed in Arabic. The Roman character is coming into use. Hindustani is the language of the Muhammadan rather than of the Hindu population. It is not peculiar to any district.

282. URDU (Persian char.). (*North India.*)

کیونکہ خدا نی جہان کو ایسا پیار کیا ہی کہ اسنی
اپنا اکلوتا بیٹا بخشا تا کہ جو کوئی اسپر ایمان لاوی
ہلاک نہووی بلکہ ہمیشہ کی زندگی پاوی

In South India Hindustani differs somewhat from that in the north, and is called Dekhani.

The number speaking Urdu may be roughly estimated at 25 millions.

The following table shows the resemblances between a few very common words belonging to some of the principal languages of the Northern Family:

	Bengali.	Hindi.	Urdu.	Marathi.	Gujarati.*
Man	manusha	manas	mard	mansh	mánus.
Eye	chhakyuh	ankh	ànkh	doleh	ànkh.
Ear	karna	kàn	kàn	kan	kàn.
Nose	†	nàk	nàk	nakh	nàh.
Mouth	mukh	mukh	munh	tond, mukh	mohodum.
Tooth	danta	dant	dànt	dant	dànt.
Hand	hàt	hàth	hàth	hàt	hàth.

* From Latham's *Comparative Philology.* † Not given by Latham. The accents also are, in most cases, not given.

BENARES GENTLEMAN.

BENARES LADY.

Daily Life.—As in other parts of India, cultivation is the chief employment of the people. When there was a failure

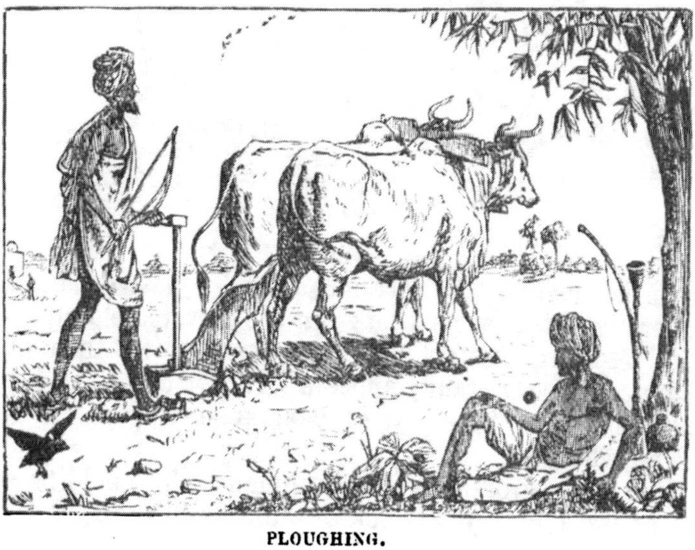

PLOUGHING.

of rain formerly millions perished from famines. Such are now mitigated by numerous canals from the great rivers, and by railways enabling grain to be transported. The cattle, as well as the men, are larger than in Bengal. During the cold season they are sometimes protected by coverings.

The common native mode of travelling is by bullock or horse *ekka.* The body of the carriage is set upon two wheels, without any springs, so that on bad roads there is a good deal of jolting. A horse has often a number of small bells suspended from its neck, which make a jingling noise

EKKA.

when it moves. The carriages used by native ladies are generally of the same kind; but are covered closely over with a screen, often of red cloth, which gives them at a distance a rather gaudy appearance. No one can see the ladies inside; but they can peep out at small apertures, and see all who pass.

There are several tribes of Brahmans, who would be put out of caste if they partook of a meal sitting together on the same mat. Sir W. W. Hunter saw a Brahman felon try to starve himself to death, and submit to a flogging rather than eat his food, on account of scruples as to whether the birth-place of the North-Western Brahman, who had cooked it, was equal in sanctity to his own.

Nautches are noticed here, though the evil prevails, more or less, all over India. The *Subodh Patrika* has the following remarks on them :

" Not the least urgent of such subjects of reform is the institution of dancing girls among us. Stripped of all their acquire-

DANCING GIRL.

ments, these women are a class of prostitutes pure and simple. Their profession is immoral and they live by vice. Being never married they can never be widows. Hence the wedding tie woven by these women is considered propitious and sufficiently potent to confer life-long wifehood on the newly-married girl. Indeed their presence at marriage and other ceremonies is almost a necessity, and few persons who can afford the expense and are unable to disregard the opinion of their neighbours can forbear to call them to grace the occasion. The dancing girl is everywhere. It is she who crowns all merriment at all times. If it is a marriage, she gives the finishing stroke to the gaieties of the occasion. If you begin to occupy a house newly built, the ceremony of the day is only brought to a conclusion when the house rings to the noise of her anklets, as the phrase goes. Nay, you cannot treat a friend or bid farewell to a departing Anglo-Indian except by her mediation."

Her immoral influence is thus described:

"She is the bane of youthful morality. In her rich dress, her trained voice, and the skilful manipulations of her hands and feet, she is the centre of attention to young, impressionable minds. If their introduction to her is too early, there is yet no repulsion about it. And the favourable impressions thus early associated with her grow and develop with advancing years. Thus immorality is handed down from father to son."

Some of the songs sung by the women are highly objectionable. That they should be lewd is to be expected; but this is not the only blot. The *Deccan Times* quotes the following specimen: "Darling, I do not know whom to admire most, God who made you or you who were made by God! No, no, you are the more loveable! The Almighty now repents that he has created you so beautiful, O envious, jealous God!" &c.

Very large sums are often squandered on these women by men who will not give a pice for female education.

Reformers everywhere should turn their attention to this wide-spread evil, and try to check it in every possible way. They should never countenance nautches by their presence, and try to convince those who encourage them of the error of their conduct.

Religion.—Hindustan is the chief seat of Hinduism, and here Buddhism originated. Benares, or Kasi, is the most noted place of pilgrimage in India. Muttra is the supposed birth-place of Krishna, where he stole the clothes and sported with 16,000 Gopis. His history is given in the Prem Sagar. It has well been remarked: "The stories related of Krishna's life do more than anything else to destroy the morals and corrupt the imagination of Hindu youths."

RAM LILA.

The people generally believe the stories in the Prem Sagar, and see no wrong in a god being guilty of theft, adultery, and murder. The proverb is, "To the mighty there is no sin." Just as a Hindu king could take the wives of his subjects or put them to death, so it is supposed the gods may act as they please. On the contrary, for God to commit a crime would be far worse than for a man to do the same. No such being as Krishna ever existed: the story in the Prem Sagar is an invention.

Rama is largely worshipped in Hindustan. "Ram! Ram!" is a common salutation. Palky bearers use it when they take up or lay down their load. Rama is a far more nobler character than Krishna; but his fame rests chiefly on the most extravagant fables. If Rama could not hear his wife Sita when she called to him for help, much less can the prayers of his worshippers reach him. The Ramayana makes the following claim: "He who reads and repeats this holy life-giving Ramayana is liberated from all his sins and exalted with his posterity to the highest heaven." Any intelligent man can judge of the truth of this assertion.

The *Ram Lila Mela* is a favourite festival in Hindustan. A large wooden erection is made to represent a fort, in the midst of which is a huge image of Ravana, surrounded by his fellow-giants. This is shown on the right of the picture on page 71. Opposité is seen the figure of Rama wearing a crown, and bending his bow to shoot at the giants. In the enclosure are the actors of the festival, dressed as monkeys, to personate the allies of Rama, and waving torches. After a kind of representation of a battle, the images of Ravana and the other giants, with their fort, are set on fire and consumed. Ignorant Hindus believe that Ceylon, now under the King of England, is still peopled by demons.

Literature.—Mr. A. Grierson has given a list of 950 Hindu authors who flourished between the twelfth century A.D. and the present time. He says: "As far as my information goes, the earliest vernacular literature of Hindustan is the bardic chronicles of Rajputana. The first bard of whom we have certain information was the well known Chand Bardai, who celebrated, towards the end of the 12th century, the fortunes of Prithi Raj, the Chauhan of Dílli. Ramanand, the populariser of the worship of Rama, flourished about the year 1400 ; and even greater than he was his famous disciple Kabir." Nearly every great writer of Hindustan flourished during the 16th and 17th centuries, contemporary with Shakespeare and others in England. Tulsi Das, who died in 1624, wrote the Ramayana, the most popular book in the language. About the middle of the 17th century, Behari Lal Chaube wrote *Sat Sai*, 700 verses. for each of which he received a reward of a gold *ashrafi* from King Jai Singh.

Urdu, cultivated by Muhammadans, has comparatively an extensive literature.

THE RAJPUTS.

Although the Rajputs do not form a separate nation speaking their own language, they deserve notice as one of the most distinguished races in India. Their vernacular is Hindi.

The country of Rajputana possesses an area of about 130,000 square miles, rather more than that of the Bombay Presidency. The population is about ten millions. A small district in the centre is under British Rule ; the rest is divided into eighteen Native States.

The Aravalli Hills divide Rajputana into two parts. Towards the west much of the country is a desert, with sand hills, blown about by the winds. The few wells are, in some cases, two or three hundred feet deep. The water-wheel, with rows of pots, is largely used in Rajputana. The creaking noise which it makes is often heard. Some parts of the country are comparatively fertile.

The Rajputs are generally supposed to have been a Scythian tribe from Central Asia. The aborigines of Rajputana call themselves "sons of the earth" or "children of the forest," while the Rajputs claim to be Suryas, of sun descent. The Jats and Rajputs are so like each other that they probably belonged to the same original stock.

At what date the Rajputs first entered Rajputana is unknown. When the Muhammadans invaded India, Rajput kings were ruling over extensive tracts from the Panjab to Oudh. Had these monarchs and their tribes united together firmly, they would have driven back the Muhammadans. Unfortunately they were at constant feud with one another, and, hence, gradually fell a prey to the sword of the conquerors. The tribal wars of the great Rajput houses, and

WATER WHEELS.

their eventual subjugation by a foreign foe, produced the separation and dispersion of the Rajput tribes, and led to their occupying, for the most part, new territories. Some of the chiefs entered the service of the Muhammadan Emperors, and some permitted their daughters to marry Muhammadan princes. The Oodeypore family is considered the highest in rank among the Rajput chiefs, claiming direct descent from Rama, and to belong to the elder branch of the Suryavamsa, or 'Children of the Sun.' It is the boast of the family that they never gave a daughter to any of

RAJPUTS.

the Muhammadan Emperors. Up to the time of Akbar, the Rajput chiefs, more or less, preserved their independence; but in a short time they lost this position, and became simple feudatories of the emperor. Rajputana afterwards fell almost completely under the sway of the Mahrattas, who exacted tribute, ransomed cities, annexed territory, and extorted subsidies. After severe fighting, the Rajputana chiefs were taken under British protection about 1818, and were firmly established in their territories again.

A Rajput chief rules the head of a tribe divided into numerous clans, at the head of which are petty chiefs, generally members of his own family, all of whom acknowledge his sovereignty and pay him tribute, while his own authority is only absolute over those tracts which are not in their hands or under their control. In some cases the rights of the smaller chiefs are as ancient as the right of the ruling prince to the state which he governs. The Thakurs, or great landholders, similarly claim from their dependents customary dues or services.

The Rajput population, though the first in rank and influence, number only about half a million. The Brahmans, who come next, are nearly twice as numerous.

"The poorest Rajput of this day," says Tod, "retains all the pride of ancestry, often his sole inheritance; he scorns to hold the plough, or to use his lance but on horseback. In these aristocratic ideas he is supported by his reception among his superiors, and the respect paid to him by his inferiors. The honours and privileges, and the gradations of rank among the vassals of the Rana's house, exhibit a highly artificial and refined state of society. Each of the superior rank is entitled to a banner, kettle-drums preceded by heralds and silver maces, with peculiar gifts and personal honours, in commemoration of some exploit of their ancestors." Every royal house had its palladium which was frequently borne in battle at the saddlebow of the prince. Rao Bhima Hara, of Kota, lost his life and his protecting deity together.

Sherring says: "At the present time a wide-spread

desire manifests itself among various aboriginal tribes of the Central Provinces to conform to Rajput usages, and by adopting the designation of Singh, a title peculiar to Rajputs, to elevate themselves to their rank, and so in the course of time to be generally recognised as connected with them. In this manner there is reason to believe not a few aboriginal clans have risen into Rajputs."

Some years ago a sad picture was drawn of the Rajput chiefs by Aberigh-Mackay:—

> "The children of the sun and moon, the children of the fire-fountain, seem to have forgotten the inspiriting traditions of their race, and have sunk into a state of slothful ignorance and debauchery that mournfully contrast with the chivalrous heroism, the judicious and active patriotism, the refined culture and the generous virtue of their ancestors . . . . . Hardly able to read or write his own language, ignorant of all pertaining to his race, pertaining to his State, pertaining to his sacred office as a ruler of men—the petty Rajput of the present day often saunters away his miserable existence in the society of abominable creatures that cast discredit on the name of servant. Besotted with spirits and opium, dull, morose, and wretched, he knows nothing of his affairs; and leaves everything to plundering 'Managers' and 'Deputy-Managers.' He is generally hopelessly in debt. He seldom cares for any thing but the merest shadow of his dignity, the ceremony with which he is treated. Of this he is insanely jealous. That all the honours due to royalty and Rajput blood should be paid to him; that he should be saluted with guns, and received at the edge of carpets, and followed by escorts of cavalry; that his daughters should be married at an early age to princes of higher clans than his own; that his Thakurs should attend him at the Dassehra and perform the precise ritual of allegiance—all this is what he craves."

To remedy this state of things, the Mayo College was founded at Ajmere in 1875. It is intended for the sons of princes and noblemen in the whole of Rajputana, where they may be brought into direct contact with European ideas, under healthy influences of physical and moral training. Each of the large Rajput states has its own quarters for students.

Pride is a besetting sin of Indians; but nowhere was it carried to such a length as in Rajputana. Genealogists and poets exercise a vast influence over the people. It is to them that the proudest Rajput looks for solace in adversity, and for increased joy and exultation in prosperity. These men are notorious for their rapacity as beggars, and are much dreaded by their employers on account of the power they have of distorting family history at public recitations, if they choose to do so, and of subjecting any member to general ridicule. At marriages large sums were sometimes given to them. On the occasion of a marriage between two noble families a few years ago, the bridegroom expended one and a half lakhs of rupees on such gifts alone. The marriage of a daughter in Rajputana, times without number, marked the era of the family ruin—the income of several years squandered, estates encumbered, a legacy of debt and misery handed down to succeeding generations. To avert the ruin of the family, a daughter at her birth was frequently put to death. All this happened that a senseless custom might be kept up, that one family might not seem to outdo another in the matter of display of riches, and profuse liberality. In the history of mankind is there on record a more pitiful display of human vanity?

Two centuries ago the great Maharaja Jai Singh of Jeypore took up the question of curtailing marriage expenses among the Rajputs. His plan was frustrated by the vanity of the Chandawut of Saloombra, who expended on the marriage of his daughter a sum even greater than his sovereign could have afforded. Tod says: "To have his name blazoned by the bards and genealogists, he sacrificed the beneficent views of one of the wisest of the Rajput race."

Since then there have been a number of unsuccessful attempts in the same direction on the part of individual chiefs. Unfortunately they acted independently of each other, and failures were the result. In 1887, Colonel

Walter, the British Agent in Rajputana, suggested that a large representative committee should meet at Ajmere to consider the question. The members were to consist of one official, one leading Jaghirdar, with one bard, or poet, from each State. Not only were the marriage expenses reduced; but it was agreed that throughout the whole of Rajputana boys and girls should not be married before the ages of 18 and 14 respectively. The rules laid down have, on the whole, been fairly observed. The Rajputs have thus placed themselves in the van of progress. May their example soon be followed by all others in India.

Formerly in Rajputana every town and village had its wall; every man went armed. Walls in many places are allowed to decay, and weapons are ceasing to be worn.

Christian Missions have been established in the chief cities of Rajputana, and knowledge is spreading.

MARWARIS.

Money-lenders, so called, are found in many parts of India. They belong to the Rajputana State called MARWAR, the capital of which is Jodhpur. Their language is Marwari, a dialect of Hindi. Many of them are Jains, strongly opposed to the destruction of animal life of every kind.

The peaked turban is a peculiarity of the Marwari dress. In pursuit of trade the Marwaris quit their homes for years, only revisiting them on occasions of marriages or family concerns. Although far from their Native State, they remain loyal to their chief. When the late Maharaja Takht Singh died, every Marwari in Calcutta and Bombay shaved his head as a mark of mourning.

Getting into debt is a characteristic of Hindus. Mr. M. Malabari* shows how the Marwaris profit by this weakness:

"The Marwari allows credit to his customers till it has reached, say a rupee; then begins the interest at two annas a month; then it becomes a book debt; then is required a security

---

* *Gujarat and the Gujaratis.*

—an old ring, a few cooking utensils, some wearing apparel, &c. These are lodged with the Marwari till the lodger has drawn upon the shop for about half their value. Fresh security is now required, if fresh supplies of rotten grain, adulterated oil, wet fuel, &c., are applied for. He charges heavy interest for the credit money, and he turns to account the security lodged with him. He lends the ring, the clothes, the utensils or the furniture to others, and charges for the use. If those who have lodged the articles with him object to their being used, why they must close their account with him!

"The Marwari will lend and sell on credit to the last pie compatible with safety. Infinite is his power of lending, so is his power of recovering. The moment the Marwari finds difficulty in repayment, he sets about squeezing the last drop out of the unhappy wretch. He removes from his house everything worth removing. He does not scruple to put his victims to the vilest uses, so he can recover what he thinks to be his due. When all fails to satisfy the relentless fiend, he resorts to the Small Cause Court. Those who know what a summary suit is need not be told that the Marwari has the power to sell by auction everything the debtor may possess. He often buys up every thing himself.

"The Marwari feeds upon the poorer classes of Hindus, but clerks and others likewise fall victims to his rapacity. His policy is the policy of the 'long rope.' He lends and lends till the man is completely in his power, and is virtually his slave for life."

If the Hindus would give up their wretched habit of getting into debt, they would be much richer and happier than at present.*

THE BHILS.

It is disputed whether the Bhils are an aboriginal tribe of Kolarians. They are distinguished by their dark colour, diminutive size, prominent cheek bones, large nostrils, activity, and skill as hunters. They have lost their own language and speak a kind of Hindi. Old Muhammadan

* See *Debt and How to Get out of it.*

historians allude to them as a powerful tribe, occupying the hills and forests of Southern Rajputana, from which they were driven out. Many settled in Khandesh, in the north of the Bombay Presidency. Unlike the orthodox Hindu, the Bhil has always eaten the flesh of the cow. In fact, he eats every wild animal except the monkey which is universally worshipped in the form of Hanuman. The tiger is held in great respect, and the people are very unwilling to kill it, unless it be a man-eater. If a beast has thus become obnoxious, a trial is held with religious rites, and if the animal is found guilty, sentence is passed upon him, he is pursued, killed, and hung up on a tree over the main road as a warning to all evil-doers of his species. It is very curious, and shows the antiquity of this race, that at the coronation of the highest Rajput chiefs, in states where the Bhils live, the sacred mark of kingship is impressed on the forehead of the new chief by the head of the Bhil family to which this hereditary privilege belongs, and the Bhils do not regard him as their king till this ceremony has been performed. Not even to save his life, it is said, will a Bhil tell a falsehood. Their most solemn oath is by the dog, their most valuable companion in the chase. They take every opportunity of having a feast and a drinking-bout. Their drink is made from the white flowers of the Mowra, which yield a highly intoxicating spirit. They burn their dead, except unmarried children of both sexes who are buried, as also those who die from small-pox. In case of cholera they also bury the dead, believing that the smoke from the pyre disseminates the disease. The dead are propitiated by offerings. Witchcraft and omens are implicitly believed in; charms of various kinds are universally used. The ordeal by water prevails among all the barbarous non-Aryan tribes of Central India. Here is a description of one water-test, taken a few years ago from the mouth of an expert witch-finder among the Bhils, who got into a scrape for applying it to an old woman.

A bamboo is stuck up in the middle of any piece of

water. The accused is taken to it, lays hold of it, and by it descends to the bottom. In the meantime one of the villagers shoots an arrow from his bow and another runs to pick it up and bring it back to the place whence it was shot. If the woman is able to remain under water until this is done, she is declared innocent, but if she comes up to breathe before the arrow is returned into the bowman's hand, she is a true witch and must be swung as such.

In the case from which this account is taken the woman failed in the test, and was accordingly swung to and fro, roped up to a tree, with a bandage of red pepper in her eyes; but it is obvious that this kind of ordeal, like almost all primitive ordeals, is contrived so as to depend for its effect much upon the manner in which it is conducted, whereby the operator's favour becomes worth gaining. A skilful archer will shoot just as far as he chooses.

Another mode of trial is by sewing the suspected one in a sack which is let down into water about three feet deep. If the person inside the sack can get her head above water she is a witch. An English officer once saved a witch in India from ducking to death, by insisting that the witch-finder and the accusers generally should go through precisely the same ordeal which they had prescribed. This idea hit off the crowd's notion of fair play, and the trial was adjourned *sine die* by consent.*

An interesting account of Sir James Outram's efforts to civilise the Bhils will be found in *Anglo-Indian Worthies*.† Christian Missions have been commenced among the Bhils, and already a few have been baptised.

THE SIKHS.

The Sikhs are a fine stalwart race of men inhabiting the Panjab. Their language is Panjabi. They number a little over two millions. Most of them belong to the same stock

---

* Lyall's *Asiatic Studies*, pp. 83-84.

† Price 4 as. Obtainable from Mr. A. T. Scott, Tract Depôt, Madras.

as the Jats. The Mazabi Sikhs have sprung from the village scavengers. In the Sikh wars they greatly distinguished themselves.

The word *Sikh*, corrupted from *sishya*, means disciple. It is used to express the close dependence of the sect on their Gurus or teachers.

SIKH JAT.

Nanak, the founder, was born near Lahore in the year 1469 A.D. His teaching was mainly based on that of Kabir, a Hindu reformer. Nanak's idea was to bring about a union between Hindus and Muhammadans on the common ground of a belief in one God. But the creed of

Nanak was not monotheism (belief in one God), but pantheism (belief that God is all). He taught the repetition of the name of Hari as the only means of salvation.

Nanak travelled a great deal. It is said that he could fly through the air, and if he did not wish to go to a place, he could make it come to him. He performed the pilgrimage to Mecca. On being reproved for lying down with his feet towards the Kaaba, which was considered disrespectful, Nanak inquired in which direction he could turn his feet where the same disrespect would not be offered, for God is everywhere.

Nanak died in 1539, when 70 years of age. The tenth Guru, Govind, converted the Sikhs into a nation of fighting men. He abolished caste among his followers, and they were to add *Singh* (lion) to their other names; they were to be distinguished by long hair, to carry a sword, and to wear short trousers. The greater part of Govind's life was spent in war, and at last he was assassinated. There is a temple at Patna dedicated to him. Govind refused to appoint a successor, saying "After me you shall everywhere mind the book of the Granth-Sahib as your Guru: whatever you shall ask, it will show you." The *Adi-Granth*, 'Original Records,' was translated into English a few years ago by Professor Trumpp. He considers it "an extremely incoherent and wearisome book, the few thoughts and ideas it contains being repeated in endless varieties." "It is a jumbling together of metrical precepts and apophthegms, supposed to have been composed by at least thirty-five different authors, among whom are fifteen professional panegyrists, employed to write eulogies on the Guru." Interspersed, however, there are some noble thoughts.

"The Sikhs pride themselves on the prohibition of image worship. Yet they make an idol of their own sacred book, worshipping it as truly as the Hindus do their idols, dressing it, decorating it, fanning it, putting it to bed at night, and treating it much in the same manner as the idols of Krishna are treated."

"The Sikhs observe caste, and in most respects conform

to the customs of the Hindus. They even surpass the ordinary Hindu in some of his most inveterate superstitions; as, for example, in ascribing divine sanctity to the cow. At one time in the Panjab, it was infinitely more criminal to kill a cow than to kill a daughter, meriting nothing less than capital punishment. This arose simply from opposition to the Musalmans, who, whenever they conquered any district peopled by Hindus, invariably slaughtered cows both to ratify their victories, and to show their contempt for Hindu superstitions. The Sikhs, when it was in their power, retaliated by killing pigs in mosques. Nanak intended to draw the Sikhs and Muhammadans together; but instead of that, there is bitter hatred."

Sikhs may drink wine, but they must refrain from tobacco. Its use would destroy all the merit previously acquired.

There is a class of Sikh fanatics, called *akalis*, worshippers of the timeless God. They wear a high-peaked turban, encircled by steel *chakras*, used as weapons, and on their wrists an iron ring. They believe themselves justified in putting every opponent of their religion to death. They will only eat the flesh of animals which have been killed according to a certain rule, termed *jhatka*.

Ram Singh, originally a carpenter, about 30 years ago, claimed to be a Guru, raised up to purify the Sikh religion. His disciples have ten points of faith—five affirmative and five negative.

The first are called five *Ks*, and are *Kara, Kachh, Kerpal, Kaughi, Kes*. Iron ornaments, short drawers, iron quoits or weapons, the comb, and hair. That is to say, they are not to be effeminate, nor to shave, and to be always ready for fighting.

The negative points of the faith are contained in the formula: *Nari-mar, Kuri-mar, Sri Katta, Sunnet Katta, Dhir Malia.* That is to say, they are *not* to smoke, *not* to kill their daughters, *not* to consort with or trust the crown shorn, *nor* the circumcised, *nor* the followers of the Guru of Kartarpur.

The Kukas reject altogether the Hindu Sastras; they do not drink, do not eat meat, never eat from the hand of any but a Kuka, and above all regard the law as sacred. In 1872 there was an outbreak of the Kukas, when 70 of them were executed, and their leader Ram Singh was sent as a prisoner to Burma.

The Panjabi language is considered by some to be only an old Hindi dialect; others claim it as a separate language. It employs an old character resembling Nagri, called Gurumukhi, because it was at first only employed for taking down the sayings of the Gurus. Some Panjabi books are also written in the Persian character. Panjabi is spoken by about 14 millions. One of the most popular works is the *Janam Sakhi*, a biography of Guru Nanak.

Pious Sikhs are bound to repeat every morning the *Japji*, or *Guru Mantra*, consisting of 40 slokas, written by Nanak. Sir Monier Williams thus describes his conversation with a Sikh about his prayers:

"Only the other day I met an intelligent Sikh from the Panjab, and asked him about his religion. He replied, 'I am no idolater; I believe in One God, and I repeat my prayers, called *Japjee*, every morning and evening. These prayers occupy six pages of print, but I can get through them in little more than ten minutes.' He seemed to pride himself on this rapid recitation as a work of increased merit.

"I said, 'What else does your religion require of you?' He replied, 'I have made one pilgrimage to a holy well near Amritsar. Eighty-five steps lead down to it. I descended and bathed in the sacred pool. Then I ascended one step and repeated my *Japjee* with great rapidity. Then I descended again to the pool, and bathed again, and ascended to the second step and repeated my prayers a second time. Then I descended a third time and ascended to the third step and repeated my *Japjee* a third time, and so on for the whole 85 steps, 85 bathings, and 85 repetitions of the same prayers. It took me exactly 14 hours from 5 P.M. one evening to 7 A.M. next morning, and I fasted all the time.'

"I asked, 'What good did you expect to get by going

through this task?' He replied, 'I hope I have laid up an abundant store of merit which will last me for a long time.'"

The following remarks were made to Sir Monier Williams at Amritsar:

"On leaving the temple I talked for a time with an intelligent Sikh who had received an English education. Pointing to an idol of Krishna which had been set up on the margin of the lake, I asked whether the Sikhs were returning to the worship of Vaishnava images. 'Yes,' he said, 'we are gradually lapsing into our old habits. Our first Guru abolished caste and forbad the worship of idols. Our tenth Guru was a thorough Hindu at heart, and by his own example encouraged the return to Hindu practices; so that of the Sikhs now found in the Panjab a large number adopt caste, wear the Brahmanical thread, keep Hindu festivals, observe Hindu ceremonies (such as the *sraddha*), and even present offerings to idols in Hindu temples." *

Several Sikhs have embraced Christianity. Missions are scattered over the Panjab.

The Sikh chiefs have established a college in the Panjab.

The Sikhs were the most gallant foes the English ever encountered in India, but they are now very loyal to the British Government, and during the Mutiny they rendered most essential service.

KASHMIRIS.

KASHMIR, or Cashmere, is a valley in the north-west of the Himalayas, famous for its fine climate and the beauty of its scenery. It forms a basin surrounded on every side by lofty mountains. In the centre is a tract of rich land, traversed by the Jhelum. It was a favourite resort during the hot season of the Muhammadan emperors of India. It has suffered much from earthquakes. Shawls, made of the inner hair of a species of goat, are the most noted manufacture.

* *Religious Thought and Life in India*, pp. 177, 178.

The country has passed through many changes. There was an ancient Hindu kingdom. It is remarkable for its Rajatarangini, supposed to be the only Indian History properly so called. Muhammadanism was introduced in the 14th century. In 1752 Kashmir was conquered by Ahmad Shah, and it remained under Afghan sway till 1819, when it was taken by the Sikhs. In 1846 Gholab Singh obtained possession of the province as a feudatory of the British Government. The Kashmiris are fair and handsome. Some of the women wear their hair in a peculiar way. There are three varieties of the Kashmiri language. The Brahmans use many Sanskrit words; the Muhammadans, Persian and Arabic words; the women and uneducated use the old forms.

About two-thirds of the people are Muhammadans, who have often been badly treated by their Hindu rulers. A recent Raja thought that one of his ancestors had transmigrated into a fish. To prevent his being eaten, the use of fish as an article of food was forbidden.

The Muhammadans tell dreadful tales of the oppression which they suffered during the rule of the Sikhs. One of their sayings is, *Sikah nílu tah bándah begári*, Like a Sikh obliging one to buy what they have to sell, and compelling the musician to play without hire.*

Some Brahmans from Kashmir have settled in India, where they are known as Kashmiri pandits. A service similar to that for the dead was performed over such of them as were about to emigrate, as their relatives looked upon them as dead henceforward. The way was so long and difficult, and the means of correspondence so uncertain, that they never expected to receive tidings of the absentees, much less to welcome them back into the home circle. In time, the wanderers fell away from the customs of their house, and embraced those of the people amongst whom they had settled. Thus it has come to pass that whilst Kashmiri Brahmans domiciled in India have accepted the

* *Dictionary of Kashmir Proverbs*, by Knowles.

KASHMIRI WOMAN.

severe ritual of the Indian Brahmans in matters of food and drink; their brethren in Kashmir, whom they characterize as intolerant and ignorant, do not object to meat, will take water from a Muhammadan, eat with their clothes on, and have no repugnance to cooking and taking their meals on board a boat.

AFGHAN.

AFGHANS OR PATHANS.

The Afghans consist of various tribes, belonging to Afghanistan, but of whom nearly a million are found in British territory.

Their language, called Pashtu or Puktu, is Aryan. In its grammatical forms it most resembles Sindi. It has borrowed from Persian, Arabic, and Hindustani. Spoken by tribes in perpetual warfare and occupying inaccessible mountains and valleys, there is a great variety of dialects. The literature is rich in poetry.

AN AFGHAN BRIDE.

As a race the Afghans are athletic. often with a fair complexion, a flowing beard, generally black or brown, but sometimes red; the cheek bones are prominent; the nose is high and hooked. The hair is shaved off from the forehead to the top of the head, the remainder at the sides being allowed to fall in large curls over the shoulders. Their step is full of resolution, their bearing proud, and apt to be rough. They are passionately fond of hawking and hunting. The women have handsome features of Jewish cast (the last trait often true also of the men); fair complexions, sometimes rosy, though usually a pale sallow; hair braided and plaited behind in two long tresses terminating in silken tassels. They are rigidly secluded, but intrigue is frequent.

The Afghans, inured to bloodshed from childhood, are familiar with death, bold in attack, but easily discouraged by failure; excessively turbulent and unsubmissive to law or discipline; apparently frank and affable in manner, especially when they hope to gain some object, but capable of the grossest brutality when that hope ceases. They are unscrupulous in perjury, treacherous, vain, and insatiable, passionate in revenge, which they will satisfy in the most cruel manner even at the cost of their own lives. Nowhere is crime committed on such trifling grounds, or with such general impunity, though when it is punished, the punishment is atrocious. Some of the tribes are pastoral, wandering about with their cattle; others are agricultural, settled in villages.

The men of the section of a village having come to a decision, send their representatives to a council of the whole village, and these again to that of the sept (*khel*), and the appointed chiefs of the septs finally assemble as the council (*jirgah*) of the tribe. These meetings, in all their stages, are apt to be stormy. But when once a council has decided, implicit compliance is incumbent on the tribe, under heavy penalties, which the *maliks* or chiefs have the power of enforcing. Justice is administered in the towns more or less effectively, according to Muhammadan law, by a *kázi* and *muftis*. But the Afghan communities are chiefly guided by a rude system of customary law. A prominent law in this code is that called 'entering in.' By this law the Pathan is bound to grant any boon claimed by the person who passes his threshold and invokes its sanctions, even at the sacrifice of his own life and property. So also, the Pathan is bound to feed and shelter any traveller claiming hospitality. Retaliation must be exacted by the Pathan for every injury or insult, and for the life of a kinsman. If immediate opportunity fail, a man will watch his foe for years, with the cruel purpose ever uppermost, using every treacherous artifice to entrap him. To omit such obligations, above all blood revenge, exposes the Pathan to scorn. The injuries of one generation may be avenged in the next, or even to remoter posterity. The relations of a murdered man may, however, before the tribunal council, accept a blood-price. The crimes punished by the Pathan code are such as murder without a cause, refusal to go to battle, disobedience to the decision of a tribal council, adultery. To guard against revenge, they are generally armed, even when grazing cattle, driving beasts of burden, or tilling the soil.

The Afghans are Muhammadans of the Sunni or orthodox body, with the exception of a few tribes, perhaps not truly Pathan, who are Shias. They are much under the influence of their *mallas*, especially for evil, and have a stronger feeling against the Shia heretic than against the unbeliever, their aversion to the Persians being aggravated thereby. But to those of another faith, they are more tolerant than most Muhammadans, unless when creed becomes a war-cry.

Afghanistan has from time to time been, and is now, under one prince, but it is hardly a monarchy as we are wont to understand the term. It is rather the government of a dictator for life over a military aristocracy, and within this, a series of small democracies. The *Sardars* govern in their respective districts, each after his own fashion; jealous, ambitious, turbulent, the sovereign can restrain them only by their divisions. There is no unity or permanence. In war, as in peace, chiefs and soldiers are ready to pass from one service to another without scruple. When an old Afghan was told of the advantages of quiet and security under a strong king, he replied: "We are content with discord, we are content with alarms, we are content with blood, but we will never be content with a master."

The Khyber Pass to the west of Peshawar, is long, rugged, narrow, and winding, often enclosed by precipitous and perpendicular walls of rock. The Khyberis wear a dark turban, a dark blue coat and sandals of straw; their arms are a sword, a short spear, and a matchlock, with a wooden fork to serve as a rest. They were hereditary robbers, levying blackmail or plundering travellers through the pass. Upon the steep hills, they could throw down stones or fire upon the people below, who were unable to defend themselves. The tribes were proverbially faithless to their engagements; being constantly tempted by the hope of booty to attack parties whose safety they had previously guaranteed. The British Government has made a treaty with them by which they agree for a certain sum every year to keep the pass open and protect travellers.

Some of the tribes are so ignorant of the religion they profess that they cannot tell even the name of their prophet. It is their great desire to have the tomb of a saint in their village. He causes rain to come, and does other good things. Pilgrims come to visit it, and make offerings. Some years ago the Afridis killed a holy man who lived among them that they might have this coveted possession.

Among the rude tribes to murder a Kafir or unbeliever is considered a passport to heaven, and the man executed for it is thought to die a martyr. The following story is an example:

"Not long ago, in the Peshawar district, a man went so very far to the bad as to shoot a Mullah. It might have been an accident, or he mistook his man, or pure villany; any how the Mullah died, and, like many another outlaw, the murderer had to fly over the border. First he tried Buneyr, but the news had preceded him; and he was refused shelter. He then tried the Swat Valley, with no better success—the country of the Akhund would have none of him. Even the Afridis, small reverence as they pay to spiritual advisers, would have nothing to say to a ruffian whose hands were dyed with the blood of a pious man. Wearied at length of being hunted from tribe to tribe, he bethought himself of repentance. 'None of you will have me,' he said, 'I can but be a martyr; I will go and kill a Sahib.' So back he came to Peshawar Cantonment, and walked down the

Mall to look for a victim. Not finding one handy, he turned off and went for a cavalry sergeant in difficulties with a troublesome horse, at whom he took deliberate aim. As luck would have it, the first bullet was stopped by a range finder the sergeant had on him, but before the latter could go for his assailant the

AFGHANS.

Pathan got another bullet through the sergeant's helmet and made a bolt for it. A plucky native ran in, and the man was ultimately secured, tried by the Commissioner the same evening, and under summary powers hanged the next morning."

A Chief Justice of Bengal and Lord Mayo were both

assassinated by Pathans for some fancied wrong done to them by other Englishmen.

Afghans often visit India as traders. Many of them are notorious for their want of cleanliness.

BALUCHIS.

Baluchistan lies south of Afghanistan, and is now under the Government of India. There are about two lakhs of Baluchis in British territory. Many of them are in Sind, which was under Baluchi Amirs before it was taken by the English.

There are several Baluchi dialects. There is no peculiar character. The Arabic character has been adopted for such printed works as have appeared.

In their own country, the Baluchis generally live in tents. They are made, like those of the Afghans, of coarse black cloth, stretched over a frame of wicker-work.

A nation that lives in tents must needs be pastoral, and it is well if it be not predatory also. No Baluchi is free from the character of a robber; least of all the Baluchi of the west. Mounted on camels, frugally furnished with dates, bread and cheese, and a little water in a leather bag, the robbers ride on, with as few stoppages as possible, till they come within a few miles of the spot upon which the attack is determined. Here they rest their camels. At night they remount, accomplish the small remainder of their journey, and make their merciless attack. The spoil being attained, they prefer to return home by a fresh route; always returning expeditiously. The lot of the slaves whom they have taken is at first very miserable. They are blindfolded as soon as caught, and tied on the camel that conveys them to the country of their future masters. The women's heads and men's beards are then shaved, and the hair extirpated with lime. This is to disgrace them in the eyes of their countrymen, should they succeed in returning to them. When once made safe, they are better treated.

The Baluchi, says Captain Burton, is far superior to the common Sindi in appearance and morals. He is of fairer complexion, more robust frame, and hardier constitution. He has his own ideas of honour, despises cowardice as much as any belted knight in the dark ages, and has no small portion of national pride and aristocratic feeling. At the same time he is violent, treacherous, and revengeful, addicted to every description of debauchery, dirty in person, rough and rude in manners. His amusements are chiefly drinking and field sports; he considers hawking or breaking a horse a far nobler occupation than reading and writing; and would rather be able to cut a fat sheep in two with his sword than master all the sciences of Bagdad and Bokhara. In consequence of this there is scarcely a single learned Baluchi in Sind. Even the princes contented themselves with an imperfect knowledge of Persian, with writing books of poems, composed for them, and sending westward for books never to be perused. One of the chiefs of the Talpur family told me, in the true spirit of the middle ages, that he himself could not write, but that he never went about the country without a munshi who could.

The Baluchi is allowed the usual number of wives; he can contract a kind of left-handed marriage with as many as four lawful concubines, and may have children by any number of female slaves. The latter must have been duly paid for, inherited, or taken in warfare, provided that in this case they refuse to become Moslems. Polygamy is not common except among the highest classes.*

An English traveller thus contrasts the Afghan and Baluchi:

"In fighting, the Baluchi dismounts and pickets his mare, and then dashes into the fray sword in hand. The Pathan fires his matchlock or rifle at long ranges, if possible from behind a rock or tree, and seldom closes with the enemy for a hand to hand fight. An Afghan, with a blood feud, is not above murdering his enemy as he sleeps. The Baluchi prefers to kill his man from the front; the Pathan from behind."

---

* Burton's *Sindh*.

SINDIS.

Sindis inhabit a province, about twice the size of Oudh, on the lower course of the Indus. Much of it is a barren desert, cultivation being generally confined to the banks of the river. In some parts the ranges of sand hills succeed one another like vast waves. The population, which is very mixed, is about 2½ millions.

SINDIS.

The Sindi language is spoken by nearly four millions in Sind and the Panjab. It has preserved more of the old forms, and is therefore more intricate and difficult than any other Aryan language. Beames says: "Whereas Hindi is satisfied with three forms of the genitive particle, Panjabi with four, Gujarati requires nine, and Sindhi twenty. It has four sounds peculiar to itself, and as its geographical position would lead us to expect, it forms a link between the Persian and Indian languages." The language has a considerable amount of literature. Several characters are in use. The Muhammadans introduced the Arabic character, with additional letters to suit the Sindi sounds. The Hindus kept up a variety of local characters, varying from time to time. Some books have been printed in Gurmukhi. Government has tried to introduce a modified Nagri.

250. SINDHI.

چا کان تہ خُداءِ جهان کي اِهڙو پِيارو رکيو جو پهنجو
هِڪڙوئي جڻِيل پُٽُ ڏناءِ تہ جيڪو تنهِ تي ويساهُ
آڻي سو جٽُ نہ ٿِئي ويترِ هميشه جِئڻُ لهي

Burton gives the following account of the Sindis; but it was written 40 years ago, and no doubt since then there has been considerable improvement.

The Sindi proper is a taller, stronger, more robust and muscular man than the native of Western India. His features are regular, and the general look of the head is good; the low forehead and lank hair of India are seldom met with in this province. The beard, especially upon the upper classes, is handsome. In *morale* he is decidedly below his organisation; his debasement of character being probably caused by constant collision with the brave and hardy tribes who have always treated him as a serf, and by dependency upon Hindu shroffs and banyas, who have robbed and impoverished him as much as possible. His chief occupations at present are cultivation, fishing, hunting, and breeding horses, camels, and sheep.

The Sindi does not in general dress so handsomely as the natives of India. Moslems in this province wear little gold about their person except a ring or seal. The old usually shave off the hair, according to the ancient practice of Islam; the young take no small pride in their long locks, which are parted in the middle of the head, curled and allowed to hang down to the shoulders, or tied up in a knot under the cap or turban. The grey beard is dyed with henna, to which a little alum is added in order to deepen the colour; young men sometimes stain the hands and feet with it. The peculiar Sindi hat, which has been compared to a European hat inverted, came into general use under the Baluchi princes. It is now worn by all but religious characters who prefer the turban. The square hat belongs to the higher and wealthier classes. The lower orders prefer clothes dyed with indigo to white dresses, as the latter show the dirt too much; some of them, especially the faqirs, affect green colours.

SINDI MUHAMMADAN MUFTI.

They have several amusements.

Kites are flown by all classes, high and low. Betting on pigeons is peculiar to the higher classes. A pigeon of the best breed is selected and trained to tumble, or turn over in flying when thrown up by the hand. Unless the pigeon tumble seven times the bet is void. A small bird is taught to fight like the quail in Afghanistan. Boys are very fond of this amusement, and have invented a number of different terms to distinguish between the several kinds of birds. Cockfighting is common. The birds are generally fought by Moslems on Friday. The Sindis are very fond of fighting rams. The price of a good one is from Rs. 15 upwards.

The Sindis are one of the most gambling of oriental nations; all sexes and orders appear to have an equal passion for play, the result, probably, of early habit. As the women are very fond of games of chance, and are skilful players, the children, who are exceedingly quick in early youth, soon learn to imitate their mothers. A boy of seven years thus becomes well grounded in all the mysteries of gambling. By constant practice he learns all the popular games of cards, dice, cowries and pice, and devotes the whole of his time to them. The Sindi is an eager player, even when there is no betting; he is insolent when winning, and sulky if he loses; quarrelsome about disputed points, and perpetually cheating.

The Sindi women are of fairer complexion than those of Western India, but are not so delicately formed. Few can read, and still fewer can write their own language. To read the Koran without understanding it is considered a feat, and in a large town not more than four or five women would be able to spell through a Persian letter. The usual Moslem prejudice against female education is strong in Sind. All are agreed upon one point, *viz.*, that their women are quite bad and cunning enough, without enlarging their ideas and putting such weapons as pens into their hands. In manners the Sindi female wants the mildness of the Indian and the vivacity of the Persian.

The women are devotedly fond of flattery and find no description of it too gross or ridiculous. Their peculiar ornament consists of large ivory rings, covering the forearm; these are worn by all sects and classes. Many of the women take snuff, and almost all smoke tobacco.

About three-fourths of the Sindis are Muhammadans. In 1859, the Province contained only 20 Government Schools: in 1884 they had increased to 340, with 23,273 pupils.

There are Mission High Schools at Karachi and Hyderabad, and some Sindis have become Christians.

Sind is growing in importance. Karachi has become one of the principal ports in India.

CUTCHIS.

Cutch, properly Kachh (sea-coast land), is a long narrow semicircular peninsula, to the north of the Gulf of Cutch, and separated from Sind by a shallow salt lake, called the Great Runn or Rann, from *aranya,* desert. It contains about 6,000 square miles, and the population is about half a million. The capital is Bhuj, where the Rao, or Chief, resides.

The most striking physical feature of Cutch is the salt desert, stretching along the north and east of the State, and one-half larger. It is believed to have been a bed of the sea, raised by some natural convulsion, and cut off from the ocean. It is now a sandy hollow, covered with water during the rains and south-west monsoon; but dry at other periods and incrusted with salt. There are some islands. Except a stray bird, a herd of asses, or an occasional caravan, no sign of life breaks the desolate loneliness.

Two ranges of hills run from east to west. The country is generally barren; but there is some good arable land upon which grain and cotton are raised. Cutchi is a dialect between Sindi and Gujarati. It is merely colloquial, Gujarati being used in literature and business.

From its isolated position, the special character of its people, their peculiar dialect, and their strong feeling of personal loyalty to the ruler, the peninsula of Cutch has more of the elements of a distinct nationality than any other Native State under the Bombay Presidency.

The greater portion of the inhabitants of Cutch seem to have come from Sind and Rajputana. The Jarejas Rajputs, the chief ruling race, claim to be descended from Krishna. They were notorious for infanticide. The explanation given is that a powerful Raja of their caste had a very beautiful daughter, for whom he asked his family Brahman to find a suitable husband. After travelling over many countries he returned unsuccessful. The Brahman then advised the Raja, to avoid the disgrace of having an unmarried daughter, to put her to death. To remove the Raja's scruples, the Brahman agreed to bear the sin, and the Raja consented. From that time it is said that female infanticide was practised by the Jarejas. Avarice and pride were the real causes.

A common way of putting the child to death was by means of opium. In some cases it died of neglect. When a person asked a Jareja the result of the pregnancy of his wife, he would, if it were a female, answer, "Nothing," an expression well understood, and used with the utmost levity. About the year 1809, Colonel Walker, Resident at Baroda, tried to induce the Jareja Rajputs to give up this inhuman practice. Jonathan Duncan, Governor of Bombay, also used all his influence, and, in course of time, the Rajput chiefs consented. In 1842 the proportion of males to females in the Jareja tribe was found to be as 8 to 1; in 1881 it stood as 2¼ to 1.

THE JAINS.

The Jains are a religious sect, not a nationality, and they have been partly noticed under the Marwaris; but as they are a numerous and interesting class in Western India, a fuller account may be given of them. They numbered in 1901 about 13½ lakhs.

The Jains are generally called Shrawaks (hearers) in Gujarat. Like the Buddhists, they have invented a succession of 24 saints, called *Tirthankars*, who have risen in the world as great religious teachers, and passed away to Nirvana. The last two were Parswanath and Mahavira. The Jains are divided into two sects, the Swetambara, or white-robed; and the Digambara, or sky-clad. These names are believed to have dated from the two last Tirthankars. Parswanath is said to have wound a white sheet round his person, while Mahavira went entirely naked. At present the Diganibar priests only lay aside their clothes at meals. The difference between the two sects is said to extend to 700 points of doctrine and practice, all of the most trivial kind, although 84 of them are regarded by the Jains as of the last importance.

The Jains, like the Buddhists, are atheists. Some time ago the head of a Jain monastery challenged the whole world to prove that there is a Creator.

The leading article of their faith is to abstain from taking animal life. Pinjrapoles, places where old cattle, dogs, birds, &c., are maintained, are supported chiefly by Jains. They care more to preserve the life of a dog, a hen, a diseased and decrepit horse, even of an ant, a bug or flea, than the life of a man. When Kathiawar came under British jurisdiction, the Jains stipulated that cattle were not to be killed for the English troops; but female infanticide had existed for untold generations without any effort on the part of the Jains to check it.

The Jains are enjoined not to eat in the open air after it begins to rain nor in the dark, lest they might unconsciously swallow a fly. They must not leave a liquid open lest an insect should be drowned. *Vayu Karma* is keeping out of the way of wind lest it should blow insects into the mouth. The priests carry a broom to sweep insects out of the way of harm, as they walk or when they sit down, and a mouth cloth to prevent insects entering the mouth.

The cots of the Jains are often infested with bugs, as they will not kill them. Some of the richer Jains pay poor men to lie for a time in their beds, allowing the bugs to feed on them, that they may not be troubled when they go to sleep.

The Jains look upon themselves as very meritorious on the above account, though many of them are extortioners, and oppress greatly those who come within their power.

Temple building is a work of great merit among the Jains. The hill Satrunjaya, near Palitana, in Kathiawar, is covered with them. Some are built of stone, others of marble. In a dark recess of each temple a marble image of one of the Tirthankars is placed, dimly lighted by a silver lamp. The eyes, made of silver, overlaid with pieces of glass, peer from every temple like those of so many cats. The silence, except at festival seasons, is very striking. Now and then in the morning a bell may be heard for a few seconds or the beating of a drum for a short time; but during the after part of the day the only sounds are those of vast flocks of pigeons that rush about from the roof of one temple to another. Squirrels and parrots abound, and peacocks are occasionally to be met with on the outer walls.

GUJARATIS.

Gujarati is the vernacular of about ten millions, chiefly inhabiting the districts around the Gulf of Cambay. The country is watered by the Tapti, Narbada, and other rivers. A great part of Gujarat is so fertile that it has been called the "Garden of India." The black soil is largely used for cotton crops. Bajra, a kind of millet, is the principal grain. A fine breed of cattle is found in the north.

GUJARÁTI. (*Western India.*)

કેમકે દેવે જગત પર એવડી પ્રીતિ કિધી, કે
તેણે પોતાનો એકાકીજનિત પુત્રએ સારૂ આપ્યો
કે, જે કોઈ તે પર વિશ્વાસ કરે તેનો નાશ ન
થાએ, પણ અનંત જીવન પામે.

The language is like Hindi; but has a little more Persian. It has three genders. The alphabet is derived from the Nagri, omitting the top line.

People.—The Brahmans of Gujarat are mostly Gurjars,

belonging to the fifth great branch of Dravida Brahmans. They have professedly 84 clans. A large proportion of them are officials in the Government service. They are also found as priests of temples or of villages and families, landowners, headmen, and even as cultivators.

There are several tribes of Rajputs especially in the peninsula of Kathiawar. The Jareja Rajputs drink wine and spirits, and partake of most kinds of animal food, except the flesh of the cow. They hold their domestic priests in little estimation. At their funerals, on the twelfth day of mourning, the priest is placed on the cot of the deceased whom he simulates. He is taken up and borne to the spot where the Jareja was burnt, the relations of the deceased following in the procession as in a real funeral. The crowd, however, pelt the unfortunate priest with stones and every available missile, so that he is obliged to leave the cot and to fly precipitately for safety. The intention of this violence is to frighten away the evil genius. This ceremony is also practised by other tribes.

Like the Jarejas of Cutch, they formerly practised female infanticide; but it has been suppressed by the British Government.

There are several agricultural tribes, who are, in general, industrious, well-clad, and live in comfortable dwellings. One class of Kunbis has the singular custom of celebrating their marriages only on one particular day of the year. The Kunbi is fond of asserting his independence. The following are some of his proverbs: "Wherever it thunders, there the Kunbi is a landholder"; "Crores follow the Kunbi, but the Kunbi follows no man."

The Banyas are mostly Jains in religion. Their evil influence over the poor cultivators, to whom they are ever ready to lend money, is well known. There are, however, honourable exceptions.

The Dhers are an extensive tribe scattered over Gujarat. They carry the baggage of travellers, act as village scavengers and occasionally as village watchmen. Spinning and weaving are their principal occupations. Although they stand in the lowest division of the scale of Hindu caste, its laws are no less binding on them than with those who stand higher. The following story is told in Gujarat:

A Muhammadan sovereign asked his Hindu minister which was the lowest caste of all. The minister begged for leisure to consider his reply, and having obtained it, went to where the Dhers lived, and said to them: "You have given offence to the Padishah. It is his intention to deprive you of caste, and make you Muhammadans." The Dhers, in the greatest terror, posted off in a body to the sovereign's palace, and, standing at a respectful distance, shouted at the top of their lungs: "If we've offended your majesty, punish us in some other way than that. Beat us, fine us, hang us if you like, but don't make us Muhammadans." The Padishah smiled, and turning to his minister, who sat by affecting to hear nothing of the matter, said: "So the lowest caste, is that to which I belong!"

The Bhangis are scavengers. They are below the Dhers in social rank, who will neither eat with nor intermarry with them. They will feed on animals that have died a natural death. The language used by them is Hindustani.

Religion.—To their disgrace, a number of Gujaratis belong to the infamous Vallabha sect of Vaishnavas. Their chief priests, called Maharajas, are regarded as incarnations of Krishna. Men and women prostrate themselves at their feet, offering them incense, fruits, and flowers, and waving lights before them. It is believed that the best way of propitiating Krishna in heaven is by ministering to the sensual appetites of the Maharajas. Body, soul, and property (*tan, man, dhan*), are to be wholly made over to them. Women are taught to believe that the highest bliss will be secured to themselves and their families by intercourse with the Maharajas. Rich Bombay merchants, as shown at a trial in 1862, gave their wives and daughters to be prostituted as an act of religious merit to men who had ruined their health by debauchery.

Mr. Malabari gives the following as some of the taxes which Maharajas exact from their wealthy followers:

For homage by sight, Rs. 5; for homage by touch, Rs. 20; for the honour of washing the Maharaja's foot, Rs. 35; for the credit of swinging him, Rs. 40; for the glory of rubbing sweet unguents on his body, Rs. 42; for the joy of sitting with him, Rs. 60; for the bliss of occupying the same room, Rs. 50 to 500; for the performance of the circular dance, Rs. 100 to 200; for the delight of eating the *pan supari* thrown out by the Maharaja, Rs. 17; for drinking the water in which the Maharaja has bathed, or in which his foul linen has been washed, Rs. 19.*

There are Christian Missions in different parts of Gujarat.

THE PARSIS.

In 1901 the Parsis in India numbered about 94,000. They derive their name from Persia, their original country. In the middle of the 7th century of the Christian era, the Muhammadans conquered Persia. Fire temples and other sacred places were destroyed or converted into mosques, and nearly the whole population embraced the faith of Islam.

Several emigrations took place. The first port in India to which refugees arrived was Diu, a small island in the Gulf of Cambay. After some stay there, they went to Sanjan, north of Bombay, where they landed about 717 A.D. Representing themselves as worshippers of the cow, they were received with favour by the Hindu Raja. They were, however, required to adopt the language of the country, to wear no armour, &c. For several centuries they lived peaceably with the Hindus. Some of them found favour even with Muhammadans.

A few Parsis settled in Bombay in the 17th century. In 1735 the Bombay Dockyard was founded under the supervision of Lowjee, a Parsi shipwright, and the post of master builder in the factory was filled for years by his descendants.

---

* *Gujarat and the Gujaratis*, p. 122.

Sir George Campbell describes the features of the Parsis as in the main of a high Aryan type, somewhat intermixed perhaps after a very long residence in India; still there is generally the prominence of feature which we might expect from an extraction originally Persian. Their language, called Parsi-Gujarati, contains a larger infusion of Persian than ordinary Gujarati.

A PARSI, MR. H. P. CAMA.

When a Parsi mother is seized with the pains of labour, she is conveyed to the ground-floor of the house, where she remains for forty days, at the end of which, after purification, she is allowed to appear in the family as before. The exact date of the birth of the child is noted, and an astrologer prepares his horoscope. When the child is seven years of age, he is invested with the sacred shirt and cord of 72 threads.

At home a Parsi wears a long muslin shirt and girdle, with a waistcoat of white cloth, loose trousers, slippers, and a skull cap. When going abroad he puts on a loose coat, and a dark coloured turban of a peculiar shape.

The Parsi women are generally fair in complexion and of a pleasing countenance. They are robbed of part of their beauty by the custom of concealing their hair under a white cloth. Their dresses are generally bright coloured, sometimes embroidered or fringed with gold lace. They are not secluded like Hindu women, and walk about unveiled.

The Parsi mode of life may be described as half European, half Hindu. Every year advancing in civilization and enlightenment, they copy more closely English manners.

The educated and influential classes have already adopted in their domestic life the comforts, conveniences and elegancies, and also the costliness, of the European style. Their garden-houses are the best in Bombay. The reception rooms are richly decorated, while the glory of a Parsi house is to be one blaze of light. When large parties are given, the table is spread exactly in the English mode, instead of as formerly, when hundreds would be grouped upon the floor, each eating his dinner from a plantain leaf.

The custom, adopted from the Hindus, was for males to take their meals apart from the females; but many educated Parsis have returned to their ancient habit. About half the Parsis are merchants, bankers or brokers. Shrewd men of business, they are, compared with their numbers, probably the wealthiest class of the population. Unfettered by caste like the Hindus, they are free to travel wherever they please.

The Parsis have shown a very praiseworthy zeal in the cause of education. Many of them have also been distinguished for their philanthropy. Others "squander away large fortunes in luxury and debauchery, without contributing a penny towards any charitable fund for objects of

TOWER OF SILENCE.

public utility."* Mr. M. Malabari, the leading social reformer in India of the present day, is a Parsi.

There are complaints that the younger Parsis are not so temperate as their forefathers. Numbers of Parsis are liquor sellers. The fondness of some for theatricals is another unfavourable symptom. The leading men should seek to check these evils.

Religion.—The Parsis are followers of Zoroaster or Zarathustra. Their sacred book is called the Avesta. It is a mixture of monotheism, dualism, and polytheism; but the intelligent among them are monotheists. Ahura Mazda, the chief divinity of the Avesta, was originally the same as the Varuna Asura, of the Veda. Ahura is the Zend form of Asura, which means *lord; Mazda* means *the knowing one.* In later times another eternal being, called Ahriman (hurtful spirit), was added. A constant war was supposed to exist between the two.

From their reverence for fire, Parsis are sometimes called fire worshippers. A fire is kept ever burning in their temples. Water is reverenced next to fire. No refuse was to be cast into a river. Like the Hindus, they attach great purifying virtue to the urine of the cow, called *nirang*. It is brought to the house every morning. A small quantity of it is applied to the face, hands, and feet. In greater purifications, some of the liquor is sipped.

In the Avesta the earth complains that she is polluted by the burial of the dead. The Parsis do not bury their dead, but expose them in towers to be devoured by vultures. The bodies are laid in what are called "towers of silence." Each tower usually has several vultures sitting motionless round the top, with their heads pointed inward. When a corpse is brought, the vultures swoop down, and in a few minutes fly back satiated, and take up their former position.

---

* The foregoing account is abridged from *The Parsis*, by Mr. Dosabhoy Framjee.

MAHRATTAS.

MAHARASHTRA probably means the country of the Mahars, an aboriginal tribe, as Gujarashtra means the country of the Gujars. The Mahratta country may be described as an irregular triangle. The shore of the Arabian Sea, for about 330 miles, forms the base; the apex is a point about 700 miles in a north-easterly direction from Bombay, some distance beyond Nagpore. The Portuguese possessions of Damaun and Goa are the northern and southern boundaries on the coast. The strip of country, averaging about 40 miles in breadth, between the sea and the Western Ghats, is called the Konkan. The tableland of the Deccan stretches eastwards from the Ghats.

The area of the Mahratta country may be roughly estimated at 110,000 square miles. In 1881 the Mahrattas numbered about 17 millions.

179. MARÁTHI. (*Bombay Pres.*)

कां तर देवाने जगावर एवढी प्रीति केली कीं, त्याने आपला एकुलता पुत्र दिल्हा, यासाठीं कीं जो कोणी त्यावर विश्वास ठेवितो त्याचा नाश होऊं नये, तर त्याला सर्वकाळचें जीवन व्हावें.

Language.—Beames says, "Marathi is, like Gujarati and Sindhi, more complicated in its structure than the other languages. It is a copious and beautiful language, second only to Hindi. It has three genders, and owing to the great corruption which has taken place in its terminations, the difficulty of determining the genders of nouns is as great in Marathi as in German." It is said to yield one-tenth of non-Aryan words. It has admitted a number of words from Arabic and Persian, as well as from the Sanskrit. Konkani is a dialect spoken in the Konkan. The Nagari character, slightly altered, is usually employed in books. It is often called *Balbodh*. A sort of running hand, called *Modi* is generally used in common life.

MAHRATTAS.

People.—The Mahrattas are a small, but hardy and active race of men. While the Bengalis often go bare-headed, the Mahrattas are noted for their large turbans. They were never so much under Muhammadan influence as Hindus in the north, so the women have far greater liberty. Mahratta ladies move about freely unveiled.

The Mahratta Brahmans are noted for their administrative talent and acuteness. In Benares itself they are highly respected for their intelligence and knowledge. Wherever there is a Mahratta rule, Mahratta Brahmans are the brains and directing power. At first they contented themselves with the highest administrative offices under Mahratta rulers; but later, as is well known, the Peshwa and other Brahmans usurped the supreme power itself, assumed the command of armies, and openly ruled the confederacy. They were the heads of a body, of which others were but the hands guided by them.

The agricultural Kunbis are the chief tribe, the same as the Kurmis of Northern India. Though they are regarded by the Brahmans as mere Sudras, they themselves claim to rank with Kshatriyas or Rajputs. To them belongs peculiarly the name Mahratta. Altogether, the Mahrattas acknowledge upwards of 200 castes, including 34 sects of Brahmans. A comparatively high position is given to those castes who work in metals.

About the middle of the 16th century, the Mahrattas, under Sivaji, recovered the power they had before the Muhammadans invaded the Deccan. Sivaji was born in a fort, his greatness arose from his forts, and in a fort he died. From this circumstance Aurangzeb contemptuously called him "a mountain rat."

Sivaji's watchwords were, "For cows and Brahmans." He also held out to his followers the prospect of plunder. Macaulay thus describes the ravages of the Mahrattas:

"The highlands which border on the western coast of India poured forth a yet more formidable race which was long the terror of every native power, and which yielded only to the genius of England. It was under the reign of Aurangzeb that the wild clan of plunderers first descended from their mountains. Soon after his death every corner of his wide empire learned to tremble at the mighty name of the Mahrattas. Many fertile viceroyalties were entirely subdued by them. Their dominions stretched across the peninsula from sea to sea. Mahratta captains reigned at Poona, at Gwalior, in Guzerat, in Berar, and in Tanjore. Nor did they, though they had become great sovereigns, therefore cease to be freebooters. They still retained the predatory habits of their forefathers. Every region which was not subject to their rule was wasted by their incursions. Wherever their kettle-drums were heard, the peasant threw his bag of rice on his shoulder, hid his small savings in his girdle, and fled with his wife and children to the mountain or the jungle. Many provinces redeemed the harvests by the payment of an annual ransom. Even the wretched phantom who still bore the imperial title stooped to pay this ignominious blackmail. The camp-fires of one rapacious leader were seen from the walls of the palace of Delhi; another at the head of his innumerable cavalry descended year after year on the rice fields of Bengal."

In 1817, Baji Rao, the principal Mahratta prince, attacked the Poona Residency, but was defeated. Afterwards he surrendered to the British.

Religion.—The Mahrattas are Hindus; but local deities are the chief objects of worship. Pandharpur, south-east of Poona, is one of the most celebrated shrines. The part of the town where it stands is considered holy, and is called Pandharikshetra, or the holy field of Pandhari. The god is called Vithoba, or Viththal. Originally a Brahman, he is now regarded as a form of Krishna. In idols, he is represented as standing on a brick, with his arms akimbo, the hands resting on the hips.

Vithoba owes much of his popularity to the songs of Tukaram, the Mahratta national poet. Tukaram was a Sudra of the trading caste, who lived about 250 years ago. He is said to have worked many miracles, and to have ascended in bodily shape to heaven in Vishnu's car. He is now worshipped himself.

At Jejuri, 30 miles from Poona, Khandoba, a raja, is looked upon as an incarnation of Siva. He is sometimes represented with his wife on horseback, attended by a dog. A wicked custom prevails of dedicating young girls to the god's service. After undergoing a ceremonial "purification," they are branded with a heated stamp. Although nominally wives of the god, they are simply prostitutes.

At Alandi, a Brahman, called Dnyanoba, is worshipped. He is said to have caused a buffalo to speak and recite a hymn from the Veda!

Missions have been established at the principal places in the Mahratta country. The number of Mahratta Christians is steadily increasing.

Literature.—Dr. Wilson says that Marathi literature consists partly of attempts in poetry to associate the popular gods of Western India with a modified pantheism. Tukaram is the most prominent writer under this head. Poetical narratives from the Ramayana, the Puranas, love songs and tales, are other classes of works. Of late years, many translations have been made from the English.

The Registrar of books says: "Men of the present generation who generally know English, read English books. There are, indeed, men of a generation or two old who read Sanskrit and Marathi books, but they do not care much to read books on secular science. They are men of the old stamp, and according to their notions no science deserves to be so called which does not treat of the nature of God, the duties of man to Him, and salvation. Theology and transcendental philosophy is all in all with them. Ninety per cent. of such books were written by old authors, and what the men of the present generation do is simply to reprint them in their entirety or in parts. These books are very widely read and are in great demand. Even those who do not understand them, read them themselves or have them read out to them by others for the merit which is supposed to attach even to their simple reading. They often contain marvellous stories and are listened to with great interest and devotion.

"Translations or abridgments of English works, chiefly intended for cramming school children with, are the order of the day. As regards *light literature*, it has been rather plentiful. The novels are mainly devoted to the intrigues of illicit love, and very seldom treat of the nobler parts of human nature. There are better novels, but they are rare."

Reactionists.—Many of the educated Mahrattas at present exhibit the curious combination of an ardent desire for political reform, with a conservative spirit in other respects. This feeling has its stronghold at Poona, a prominent centre of political activity in India.

The patriotism of which the reactionists loudly boast is thus analysed by the *Subodh Patrika* :—

"It consists in an indiscriminate admiration of Hindu manners, customs, and institutions, and a glorification of their ancestors of whose real history, however, we know next to nothing. This is associated with an uncontrollable desire to find fault with the institutions and manners of Europeans, and especially of our English rulers. To such an extent is this hallucination carried, for we can regard it as nothing better, that these people will not allow Europeans a superiority even in the physical sciences. In the Anglo-Vernacular organ of the body published in Bombay, it was stated some time ago in the vernacular columns, that the ancient Hindus had such a perfect knowledge of the laws of the physical world and such a command over nature that they could at any time and in any place they chose bring down rain. It would be worth all the energy that the reactionists can bring to bear on the task and all the money they can spend on it, to discover this once known but now, unfortunately for mankind, hidden art and publish it again to the world."

On the other hand, among the Mahrattas are some of the leading reformers in India, as Dr. Bhandarkar, the late Hon. M. G. Ranade, Mr. Chandavarkar, and others.

WARALIS.

There are several forest tribes in the Bombay Presidency; but only one can be noticed. Some years ago, the late Rev. Dr. Wilson, of Bombay, visited the Waralis, and had some conversation with them, part of which was as follows :—

After giving their own names, they were asked the names of their fathers, which were unknown to three persons.

What are the names of your wives? We never mention the names of our wives.

Did the Brahmans marry you? No, we are our own Brahmans. Our women marry us, by singing over a cup of spirits, the bridegroom drinking first, the bride second, and afterwards the whole company.

Do any of you keep more wives than one? Re! Re! We can scarcely feed one; why should we think of more?

When your wives disobey your commands, how do you treat them? We give them chastisement less or more. How could we manage them without striking them?

Do you give any instructions to your children? Yes, we say to them, Don't be idle, Work in the fields, Cut sticks, Collect cow-dung, Sweep the house, Bring water, Tie up the cows.

Don't you teach them to read or write? No Waralis can either read or write.

Do you give them any instructions about God? Why should we speak about God to them?

What God do you worship? We worship Waghia, the lord of tigers.

Has he any form? He is a shapeless stone, smeared with red lead and ghi.

How do you worship him? We give him chickens and goats, break cocoa-nuts on his head, and pour oil on him.

What does your God give you? He preserves us from tigers, gives us good crops, and keeps disease from us.

Who inflicts pain upon you? Waghia when we don't worship him. He seizes us by the throat like a cat, he sticks to our bodies.

Do you ever scold Waghia? To be sure we do. We say, you fellow, we have given you a chicken, a goat, and yet you strike us! What more do you want?

Where does the soul go after death? How can we answer that question?

THE DRAVIDIANS OF SOUTHERN INDIA.*

India, south of Maharashtra and Orissa, is chiefly peopled by nations speaking Dravidian languages. As already mentioned, they seem to have entered India from the north-west.

Bishop Caldwell reckons the Dravidian languages as twelve in number. The six cultivated dialects are Tamil, Malayalam, Telugu, Kanarese, Tulu, and Kudagu or Coorg. The uncultivated, Toda, Kota, Gond, Khond or Ku, Oraon, Rajamahal.

The following table will show the resemblances of the Dravidian languages to each other, and their unlikeness to those of the Sanskrit family :

English.	Hindi.	Tamil.	Malayalam.	Telugu.	Kanarese.
Man	manas	al	al	al	alu
Head	sar	talei	tala	tala	tale
Ear	kan	kadu	kada	chevi	kivi
Eye	ankh	kan	kanna	Kannu	kannu
Mouth	mukh	vayi	vaya	noru	bayi
Tooth	dant	pal	palla	pallu	kallu
One	ek	onru	onna	vokati	ondu
Two	do	irandu	rendu	rendu	eradu
Three	tin	munru	munnu	mudu	muru
Four	char	nalu	nala	nalugu	nalku
Five	panch	anju	anja	ayedu	ayidu

The time when the Dravidians entered India is not known with certainty ; but it must have preceded the arrival of the Aryans in the north. It has been supposed that rude tribes, like the Andaman islanders, were the first inhabitants of India. Scattered over the south of the Peninsula, there are graves, containing pottery, and stone circles, belonging to a people of whom nothing is now known. There is generally a large jar filled with human bones, sometimes partially charred, with a number of little vessels made of pottery, and with relics of iron weapons. They are sometimes found in large numbers crowded

*Under this head the compiler is largely indebted to Bishop Caldwell's *Comparative Grammar of the Dravidian Languages.*

together, without being enclosed in stone chambers, or surrounded with circles of stone, but simply embedded in the earth. The popular idea is that they were constructed by a race of men, very small in stature, but of great strength. This is incorrect, as the bones are of the ordinary size.

A brief account will now be given of the principal Dravidian Nations.

TAMILS.

A beginning is made with this language, as being probably the earliest cultivated of the Dravidian dialects, the most copious, and containing the greatest number of ancient forms. It is spoken from Pulicat, 20 miles north of Madras, and stretches along the coast to a little beyond Cape Comorin. Westward it is bounded by the Ghats. It is also the language of about one-third of the population of Ceylon. The area of the Tamil country is about 60,000 square miles, nearly the same as that of England and Wales.

Language.—Tamil is the vernacular of about thirteen millions.

269. TAMIL. ***(Karnatic and N. Ceylon.)***

தேவன், தம்முடைய ஒரேபேறான குமாரனை விசுவாசிக்கிறவன் எவனோ அவன் கெட்டுப்போகாமல் நித்தியசீவனை அடையும்படிக்கு, அவரைத் தந்தருளி, இவ்வளவாய் உலகத்தில் அன்புகூர்ந்தார்.

Although the proportion of Sanskrit in Tamil is lest than in the other cultivated Dravidian languages, is amounts to about 40 per cent. The alphabet is supposed to be derived from the early Devanagari, or from the still earlier characters that are contained in the cave inscriptions. The forms are altered by the custom of writing on the leaf of the palmyra palm with an iron stylus.

Early Civilisation.—By an examination of words which are pure Tamil, Bishop Caldwell shows that the Tamils had made some progress in civilization before the southern advance of the Aryans. They had 'kings' who dwelt in 'strong houses' and ruled over small 'districts of country.'

TAMIL SCHOOL BOYS OF THE OLD TYPE.

They had 'minstrels' who recited 'songs' at 'festivals,' and they seem to have had alphabetical 'characters' written with a stylus on palmyra leaves. A bundle of those leaves was called a 'book.' They acknowledged the existence of God, whom they styled Ko or king. They erected to his honour a 'temple,' which they called Kô-il, 'God's house.' Marriage existed among them. They were acquainted with the ordinary metals with the exception of tin, lead and zinc; with all the planets ordinarily known to the ancients, excepting Mercury and Saturn. They had numerals up to a hundred, some of them up to a thousand. They had 'medicines'; 'hamlets' and 'towns,' but no 'cities'; 'canoes,' 'boats,' and even 'ships' (small decked coasting vessels.)

"They were well versed in 'agriculture,' and delighted in 'war.' They were armed with 'bows' and 'arrows,' with 'spears' and 'swords.' All the ordinary or necessary arts of life, including 'spinning,' 'weaving,' and 'dyeing,' existed among them. They excelled in 'pottery' as their places of sepulchre show. They were ignorant, not only of every branch of 'philosophy,' but even of 'grammar.'"

The Dravidians of the south appear from the first in Sanskrit as friendly forest folk, the monkey armies who helped Rama on his march through Southern India against the demon king of Ceylon.

The People.—Bishop Caldwell says of them, "Wherever money is to be made, wherever a more apathetic or a more aristocratic people is wishing to be pushed aside, thither swarm the Tamils, the Greeks or Scotch of the east; the least superstitious and the most enterprising and persevering race of Hindus." Throughout Ceylon the coolies on the plantations are Tamils, the majority of the money-making classes in Colombo are Tamils. The majority of the domestic servants of Europeans and of the camp-followers in every part of the Presidency of Madras are Tamils.

As the Mahrattas were the great cave temple excavators, so the Tamils have distinguished themselves by the erection of the largest temples above ground.

Madras has been called "The Benighted," on account of the supposed backward condition of its people. So far as education is concerned the epithet no longer applies. The Madras Christian College, under Dr. Miller, occupies a most distinguished place, and in the matter of female education Madras takes the lead.

The late Hon. Chentsal Rau thus describes the general feeling among educated Tamils:

"Those that have been benefited by western education are either apathetic or timid. They have yet attained only the stage of agreeing in theory, but not in practice. Education has opened their eyes, but not equally so their hearts. I am, however, glad to say that they do not join the crusade against the reformers, although they do not give them any practical help. When I say this, I refer only to the general state of things; for I must admit that there are some educated men who give us their active co-operation, while again, on the other hand, there are others who, notwithstanding their high education and University degrees, have joined the opposition, and thrown all obstacles in their power in the way of reform."*

Among the few reformers may be specially mentioned R. Ragunath Rau, Dewan Bahadur, to whom Principal Wordsworth alluded as "fighting almost single-handed his strenuous battle against cruel custom and perverted erudition."

Religion.—Demon worship was the original superstition, and it has still a stronghold among certain classes, especially in the south. The majority of the demons are supposed to have originally been human beings, especially those who met with a sudden or violent death, and had been dreaded in their lifetime. All are powerful, malicious, and interfering; and all are desirous of bloody sacrifices, and frantic dances. One demon prefers the sacrifice of a goat, another a pig, a third a cock. Pariah demons require arrack in addition. Nightmare is always supposed to be caused by a demon. He seats himself on the chest of the sleeping person, and tries to suffocate him.

The devil dancer wears dresses adapted to frighten the ignorant spectators. The instruments of music are the bow, the horn, and especially bells attached to a gigantic bow. The devil dancer at last snorts and whirls about with frantic leaps. The demon has entered him, and those present

* *Indian Magazine*, 1886, p. 431.

consult him about the disease and the offerings to be made.

The spread of Jainism has already been noticed. Many of its adherents were impaled by Sundara Pandya, the reviver of the Saiva system, which was also zealously advocated by Sankar Acharya.

Ramanuja sought to depose Siva and exalt Vishnu. The Vaishnavas are mostly divided into two sects, called Tengalas (southern veda) and Vadagalas (northern veda). Their disputes often run high, sometimes leading even to bloodshed.

BELLS OF DEVIL DANCERS.

Bishop Caldwell says: "The duties of life are never inculcated in any Hindu temple. The discharge of those duties is never represented as enjoined by the gods, nor are any prayers ever offered in any temple for help to enable the worshippers to discharge those duties aright."

While there is nothing in Hindu public worship fitted to purify, in some cases there is much having a contrary influence. Connected with many of the temples in South India there are dancing girls, called *devadasis*, handmaidens of the gods. These avowed prostitutes take a prominent part in Hindu religious worship. According to the Madras Census of 1881, the number of "female dancers" in the Presidency was 11,573. It was the same with Greek worship in ancient times. The indignant words of Bishop Lightfoot may be applied to India:

"Imagine, if you can, this licensed shamelessness, this consecrated profligacy, carried on under the sanction of religion and in the full blaze of publicity, while statesmen and patriots, philosophers and men of letters, looked on unconcerned, not uttering one word and not raising one finger to put it down."

In the 16th century a number of Tamils became Roman Catholic Christians through the labours of Francis Xavier, a celebrated Missionary. The earliest Protestant Missionaries to India were sent out by the King of Denmark. They landed at Tranquebar in 1706.

Christianity has made greater progress among the Tamils than among any other Indian people. There are many self-supporting churches in different parts of the Tamil country.

Literature.—It is an interesting fact that the first Tamil word supposed to have been written is to be found in the Bible. The Hebrew term for peacocks, brought by the fleets of Solomon, is Dravidian.

Agastya is said to have first introduced Sanskrit civilization and literature in the south. "The Vindya Mountains prostrated themselves before Agastya." The legend is that he introduced philosophy at the court of the first Pandian king, wrote many treatises for his royal disciple, and now lives for ever in the heavens as the star Canopus. He is worshipped as Agasteswara, the Lord Agastya, near Cape Comorin. The people believe him to be still alive, hidden in the conical mountain of the Western Ghats, called Agastya's Hill.

Agastya is supposed to have formed the Tamil alphabet, to have written the first Tamil Grammar. He is said also to have taught the Tamils the first principles of medicine, alchemy, magic, and about fifty treatises, most of them very modern, are attributed to his pen. When a writer wished to attract attention to his work, he sought to pass it off as proceeding from Agastya.

Aryan civilization may have commenced in South India after Wijaya went from Magadha to Ceylon about the 5th century B.C.; but it did not sink deeply till many centuries later. A Chinese traveller, who visited the Tamil country about 640 A.D., mentions that the inhabitants were chiefly Digambara Jains.

The Jaina period of Tamil literature extended probably from the 8th or 9th century A.D. to the 12th or 13th. In the reign of Sundara Pandya, about the middle of the 13th century, the adherents of the Jains are said to have been finally expelled from the Pandyan country.

The greatest composition in Tamil is the Kural of Tiruvalluvar, not later than the 10th century A.D. It is said to have been the work of a poet sprung from the Pariah caste. There is nothing as an ethical treatise to equal it in Sanskrit. Two stanzas may be quoted :—

> What is the fruit that human knowledge gives,
> If at the feet of Him, who is pure knowledge,
> Due reverence is not paid?
>
> The anxious mind, against corroding thought,
> No refuge hath, save at the sacred feet
> Of Him to whom no likeness is.

The Chintamani, an epic poem containing 15,000 lines, is the most celebrated Tamil poem written by an avowedly Jain author. The style is considered superior even to that of Kamban's Tamil Ramayana. Two sets of brief verses, still largely used in schools, are attributed to Auveiyar, the reputed sister of Tiruvalluvar.

Two large collections of hymns are supposed to have been written during the Saiva revival under Sundara Pandya, the last of the old Pandyan kings. They are regarded by the Saivas as the "Tamil Veda." The same title is claimed by the Vaishnavas for their "Book of 4,000 Hymns."

Bishop Caldwell says:

"During the last 200 years Dravidian literature appears to have made but little real progress. This is sometimes attributed by natives to the discouraging effect of foreign domination, but it seems far more largely owing to the natural tendency to decay and death which is inherent in a system of slavery to the authority of great names.

"Now that native education has commenced to make real progress and the advantages of European knowledge, European civilization, and European Christianity are becoming known and felt by so many of the Hindus themselves, it may be expected that the Dravidian mind will ere long shake itself free from its thraldom, and be stimulated to enter upon a new and brighter career."

In the Madras evening bazaar, a long row of book-hawkers may be seen behind the piles of their wares. The publications sold consists almost entirely of reprints of old books. Among the people generally there is little demand for any thing else except school books.

The Press.—S. India 'is far behind the other provinces so far as the *number* of its newspapers edited by Indians is concerned. In *quality*, it takes a good position. *The Hindu*, an English daily, is one of the best native papers in India. *The Indian Social Reformer*, commenced in Madras, is an excellent paper, but it has recently been removed to Bombay.

MALAYALIS.

Malayalam is noticed next to Tamil, as an ancient offshoot, though now a good deal altered. It is spoken along the south-west coast of India from near Trevandrum to Chandragiri, near Mangalore. The name means "mountain region." In Sanskrit the country is called Kerala.

The country consists chiefly of hills and dales, intersected by streams running from east to west, and forming large back-waters connected with the sea. These, not roads, form the great medium of communication between the districts. The village system is little known, and the inhabitants live, each in his own palm garden, along the banks of the rivers and paddy lands.

Calicut, in the Malayalam country, was the first port in India where the Portuguese landed in 1498.

Language.—Malayalam is spoken by about five millions. It differs from Tamil chiefly at present by its disuse of the personal terminations of the verb, and the larger proportion of Sanskrit derivatives, which is greatest in Malayalam of the Dravidian languages. The modern character is derived mainly from the Grantha, the character in which Sanskrit is written in the Tamil country.

172. MALAYÁLAM. (*Travancore, &c.*)

എന്തുകൊണ്ടെന്നാൽ ദൈവം തന്റെ ഏകജാതനായ പുത്രനെ, അ
വനിൽ വിശ്വസിക്കുന്നവൻ ഒരുത്തനും നശിച്ചു പോകാതെ, നിത്യ
ജീവൻ ഉണ്ടാകേണ്ടുന്നതിനായി, തരുവാൻ തക്കവണ്ണം ഇത്രയും ലോക
ത്തെ സ്നേഹിച്ചു.

A dialect of Malayalam is spoken by the Muhammadans on the Malabar Coast, called Mappilas or Moplas, and by the inhabitants of the Laccadive Islands. An adaptation of the Arabic alphabet is used.

People.—Travancore, forming the south of the Malayalam country, is well called by the Brahmans *Dharma Bhumi*, the Land of Charity, for in no other part of India is so much money spent on feeding them. At one ceremony the Maharaja officiates for a short time as one of the bearers of the palanquin of the chief Brahman; he washes his feet and drinks some of the sacred water. He is a Sudra, but he is made a twice-born by passing through a golden cow or lotus. The cow is of the same weight as himself, and is afterwards distributed among the Brahmans. The Maharaja, thenceforward, cannot eat with the members of his family, but he is admitted to the high privilege of seeing the Brahmans enjoying their meals, and of eating in their presence.

The Sudras are the middle classes in Travancore. The greater portion of the land is in their hands, and, until recently, they were the principal owners of slaves. They are usually called *Nayars*, lords or masters. Their customs with regard to marriage are singular. A girl is nominally married in early youth, but it is a mere formality. When arrived at a marriageable age she accepts any suit she pleases, but the engagement is not binding on either party, and can be easily dissolved. Hence the children of a Sudra family inherit the property not of their father, but of their mother's brother. The custom of polyandry, or one woman having several husbands, is sometimes practised.

MALAYALAM LADY.

Pulayans, a slave caste, were not allowed to approach a Brahman nearer than 96 paces; a Nayar might approach but not touch a Brahman; a palmyra-climber must remain 36 paces off. Education is spreading in Travancore, and by degrees, it is hoped, caste distinctions will disappear.

Religion.—The bulk of the Malayalam people are Hindus; but Christians are more numerous than in any other part of India. In the second century a request was addressed to the Bishop of Alexandria to send Christian teachers to India. He accordingly sent Pantænus, a very learned man, who, as far as we know, was the first Christian Missionary to this country. About the 4th century a number of Syrian Christians settled along the Malabar coast. They obtained great privileges from the Rajas of Malabar, who allowed them in all matters to be governed by their own bishops. When the Portuguese came to India, they tried to induce the Syrian Christians to become Roman Catholics. Some did so; but others adhered to their ancient communion. Protestant Missions in the Malayalam country were commenced about 1816.

The Roman Catholic Malayalam Christians number about 380,000; the Syrian Christians, about 300,000.

Literature.—Malayalam literature can advance fewer claims to antiquity than the literature of any other cultivated member of the Dravidian family. With the exception of a few inscriptions on copper and stone, it commences with the *Rama Charita*, probably the oldest Malayalam poem still in existence. It was composed before the introduction of the Sanskrit alphabet now used in writing Malayalam, and exhibits the earliest phase of the language,—perhaps centuries before the arrival of the Portuguese. The bulk of the other great poems, the Mahabharata, the Ramayana, and versions of the Puranas, were composed within the last two or three centuries.

Muhammadans, called Mappilas or Moplas, number about half a million. The Madras Census Report says: "They are purely local Dravidians by blood. Among some of them there may be a strain of Arab blood from some early generation, but the mothers throughout have been Dravidian, and the class has been maintained and increased by wholesale adult conversions. Many of the Mappilas retain their Hindu law of inheritance, and they have the industrious habits of the race from which they sprang.

Along the coast they are fishermen, sailors and coolies; inland they are cultivators."

There have been several fanatical outbursts among the Mappilas.

KANARESE.

Kanarese, properly Kannadi or Karnatika, is spoken throughout the table-land of Mysore, and northward as far as Beder in the Nizam's Territory. It is also the prevailing language in Canara on the Western Coast. The area may be roughly estimated at 65,000 square miles.

Mysore contains a large number of isolated rocks, called *droogs*, from the Sanskrit *durga*, difficult of access. Many of them were used in former days as fortresses.

141. KANARESE. (*Mysore, &c.*)

ಯಾಕಂದರೆ ಅವನಲ್ಲಿ ವಿಶ್ವಾಸವಿಡುವವರೆಲ್ಲರು ನಾಶವಾಗದೆ, ನಿತ್ಯಜೀವವನ್ನು ಹೊಂದುವ ಬಗ್ಗೆ, ದೇವರು ಒಬ್ಬನಾಗಿ ಹುಟ್ಟಿದ ತನ್ನ ಮಗನನ್ನು ಕೊಡುವ ಹಾಗೆ, ಲೋಕವನ್ನು ಅಷ್ಟು ಪ್ರೀತಿ ಮಾಡಿದನು.

Language.—Kanarese is spoken by about nine millions. The alphabet is nearly the same as the Telugu. The language includes two dialects—ancient and modern—differing in their use of inflexional terminations.

People.—The Kanarese are an agricultural people. Ragi is their chief food. In disposition they are conservative. The kingdom of the mythical Sugriva, whose general, Hanuman, aided Rama, was in the Kanarese country. Vijayanagar was a great Hindu kingdom from 1118 to 1565 A.D. Vast ruins of temples, fortifications, tanks and bridges, belonging to its capital, can still be traced on the right bank of the Tungabhadra river. Last century Hyder Ali made Mysore, for a time, a powerful state.

Religion.—Jainism prevailed in the Kanarese country for several centuries towards the early part of the Christian era. In the Hassan District of Mysore there is a small town famous for its colossal image of the Tirthankar Gomatesvara. The statue is 56½ feet high, cut out of one solid block of stone. It stands on the top of a rocky hill, and can be seen for miles. The Jains say that Rishaba, their first Tirthankar, was 500 poles, about 1½ miles high! Mahavira, the twenty-fourth, degenerated to the size of a man. The statue is naked, so its maker must have belonged to the Svetambara, or sky-clad sect. Once in 20 years the great ceremony of washing the image is performed.

The Kanarese country is noted as containing the largest number of Lingayats, also called Vira-Saivas. They are a subdivision of the Saivas, worshipping only the male energy. The other Saivas associate the *yoni* with the *linga*. They are distinguished by wearing a small *linga* enclosed in a metal case. Hence they are called *Lingadharis*. Sometimes they are called *Jangamas*, from *jangama*, motion, claiming to be living symbols of the deity. The mendicants often lead about a bull, a type of the bull of Siva. *Vira* is derived from a word meaning bravery. They nearly exterminated the Jains in some parts of the Dekkan.

The Lingayat sect was founded by Basava, minister of the king of Kalyana, then a great empire stretching across the peninsula. His parents were devout worshippers of Siva. As a reward, Nandi, the bull of Siva, was born on earth as their son. The child was called Basava, the bull of the deity. On his arriving at the age of investiture, he refused to assume the Brahman thread, and would not acknowledge any *guru* except Siva. He afterwards went to Kalyana and obtained in marriage the daughter of the minister of police. When his father-in-law died, he succeeded him in his office. Various marvellous actions are ascribed to Basava and his disciples; as converting grains of corn into pearls, discovering hidden treasures, &c. When the king of Kalyana ordered the eyes of two worshippers of Siva to be plucked out, Basava left Kalyana after cursing the city, and went to a place called Sangamesvara. Through the curse of Basava, the people of Kalyana fought among themselves until the city was utterly destroyed.

Basava continued to reside at Sangamesvara, teaching his disciples. At last Siva and Parvati came forth from the Sangamesvara linga, and led Basava into the temple, and all three disappeared. Flowers fell from the sky, and the disciples made known the absorption of Basava into the emblem of Siva.

Allama Prabhu was a Brahman, regarded as a lesser incarnation of Siva. He became Basava's *guru,* and as such was concerned in the revolution at Kalyana, when the king Bijala was slain, and a new religion established.

There are Christian Missions at the principal stations in the Kanarese country ; but the languages are so mixed that it is difficult to say how many Kanarese people have become Christians.

Literature.—The Rev. F. Kittel says : " The originators of Kanarese literature are the Jains, who have cultivated both Sanskrit and the vernaculars of the South. The Sanskrit works date as far back as the beginning of the 4th century A.D. The most ancient and esteemed grammar of classical Kanarese is called *Sabdamanidarpanam* (Jewel-Mirror of Words,) written by Kesava. Most of the poets he cites were Jains." Kesava quotes eleven predecessors in the art of poetry by name, besides referring to others, and he speaks of their compositions as written in ancient Kanarese, whilst he called the language used by himself simply Kanarese, though his language is now regarded as ancient Kanarese. He flourished probably in the 12th century. Mr. Kittel says that at the time when Kesava wrote " Sanskrit words in a fixed form, either as *tatsamas* or *tadbhavas,* apparently to the same amount as in our days, had already been appropriated by the Kanarese people." Among other works the Jains wrote a Commentary on the *Amara Kosha*, called *Nachiraja*.

The Lingayats, already described, have written a number of poetical works. The *Basava Purana* is one of the most important. *Prabhu Linga Lila*, the story of Allama Prabhu, who at last ascended the Guru throne in Kalyanapura, has been translated into Tamil.

There are also Kanarese works by the Saivas and Vaishnavas.

THE NILGIRI TRIBES.

The Todas, properly Tudas, are a small tribe inhabiting the Nilgiri Hills, to the south of Mysore. They were not the original inhabitants, although the other hill tribes acknowledge them to be their superiors. There are graves scattered about the summits of the hills of which the Todas know nothing. These are raised blocks of large unhewn stone. Beneath there are earthen pots, containing ashes, pieces of half-burnt bones, images of tigers, deer, with fragments of metal resembling spear-heads, &c. The Todas permit these graves to be opened without any interference, which they would not do, were they supposed to belong to their ancestors.

The Todas are a fine, well-proportioned, powerful people, with large and sometimes aquiline nose. They are nevertheless indolent, and disinclined to work of every description. Their sole labour is watching their cattle, milking the kine, and manufacturing ghi. Their bodies are enwrapped in one long garment, their heads are uncovered; their hair both of head and beard is uncut; they are copper-coloured in complexion. The women decorate themselves with massive necklaces, and wear their hair flowing over their shoulders, though sometimes it is curled up with short sticks. They tattoo, with black dye, their necks, hands and lips in imitation of jewelry.

The language of the Todas was originally old Kanarese; but it is now more allied to Tamil than to any other dialect. They never wash their clothes and seldom their bodies, from their birth to their death. The roofs and sides of their huts are formed of twisted bamboos. The end wall is strongly built; the front wall has an opening so small that those who enter must crawl on their hands and feet.

The Todas all practise polyandry, one woman being the wife of all the brothers of a family, with each of whom

TODAS OF THE NILGIRIS.

she lives a month at a time. Formerly when the tribe was not under the British, only one female child was allowed to survive in each household.

The Todas are greatly attached to their buffaloes. On returning from the fields in the evening, these animals are saluted with much respect by their masters. Some buffaloes are held as sacred, and are never milked, but roam about with their calves at pleasure. The sacred buffalo bull is worshipped. Milk is poured before it and prayers offered by the priests by whom alone it is seen or touched. They likewise worship a hunting god, who is supposed to give them success in killing tigers. "May all be well!" is the only prayer they are heard to utter.

The funeral ceremonies of the Todas are singular. The body is burned and a great feast of slain buffaloes is given. This is called the "green funeral." Twelve months later the "dry funeral" is celebrated, but a larger number of buffaloes is killed, and friends are invited from the neighbouring tribes. An attempt was made to get some of the children to go to school; but they would not learn.

Four other tribes inhabit the Nilgiri Hills—the Badagas, Kotas, Kurumbas, and Irulas.

The BADAGAS, northmen, are supposed to have come from the north on account of famine and persecution about 300 years ago. Their language is an old Kanarese dialect. They are the most numerous, wealthy and civilised of the indigenous tribes. In 1881 they numbered 24,000; they pay tribute to the Todas.

The KOTAS are filthy in their habits and much addicted to eating carrion. They perform menial offices for the Todas and Badagas, &c.

The KURUMBAS (shepherds) collect jungle products, &c. All the other tribes stand in awe of them, and some of them officiate as priests to the Badagas.

The IRULAS, from (*irul*, darkness), live on the lowest slopes. They use animal food of every description, and are expert huntsmen.

TULUS.

Tulu is a Dravidian dialect, spoken by nearly half a million on the west coast of India, about midway between Bombay and Cape Comorin. It is destitute of a literature in the proper sense of the term, and never had a character of its own. The Kanarese character having been used by the Missionaries in the Tulu books printed by them at Mangalore—the only books ever printed in Tulu,—that character has now become associated with the language. Notwithstanding this, Tulu is one of the most highly developed languages of the Dravidian family. It differs most widely from Tamil, and least from Kanarese. All Tulu Christians are taught Kanarese as well as Tulu. Tulu, however, shows no signs of disappearing, and the people have the reputation of being the most conservative portion of the Dravidian race. The name Tulu is said to mean mild, humble.

TELUGUS.

Of all the Dravidian languages, Telugu is spoken over the largest area, and by the greatest number of people. It is current along the Eastern Coast from about Pulicat to Chicacole, where it begins to yield to Oriya. Inland it extends to about the middle of the Peninsula. Formerly, Telugu seems to have been spoken as far north as the mouths of the Ganges. There are numerous Telugu settlers in the Tamil country and in Mysore. The area may be roughly estimated at 100,000 square miles. In 1881 the number speaking Telugu was 17 millions—very nearly the same as Marathi.

Language.—The character is nearly the same as Kanarese.

The Telugu, in respect of antiquity of culture and glossarial copiousness, ranks next to the Tamil in the list of Dravidian idioms; but in point of euphonic sweetness it claims to occupy the first place. It has been styled the

"Italian of the East." Telugu, called also Telinga, is the Andhra of Sanskrit writers, a name mentioned by the Greek geographers as the name of a nation dwelling on or near the Ganges.

271. TELUGU. (*S. E. India.*)

దేవుడు లోకమును ప్రేమించుట ఏలాగంటే,
ఆయన యందు విశ్వాసముంచే ప్రతివాడును నశి
ంచక నిత్యజీవము పొందే నిమిత్తము తన జని
తైక కుమారుని ఇచ్చెను.

Of the five cultivated Dravidian dialects, the farthest removed from each other are the Tamil and the Telugu. The great majority of the roots in both languages, it is true, are identical; but they are so often disguised in composition by peculiarities of inflexion and dialectic changes, that not one entire sentence in one language is intelligible to those who are acquainted only with the other.

People.—From the earliest times the Telugu people were divided into the Andhras and Kalingas,—the former better known to the ancient Aryans. The Andhras are mentioned as early as the Aitareya Brahmana of the Rig Veda, though represented therein as an uncivilised race. In later times a dynasty of Andhra kings is said to have reigned in Northern India. Vikramaditya is said to have been a prince of the Andhra dynasty. His era, 56 A.D., is still well known. Warungal was a southern capital. In 1309 it was taken by the Muhammadans; but it recovered its independence. Between 1512 and 1543 the remains of the Hindu kingdom were annexed to the Golconda territory. The Coast Districts were acquired by the English from the Nizam in 1765.

The Telugu people were more enterprising in ancient times than at present. The Klings, who in the early centuries of the Christian era formed settlements, built temples, and exercised dominion in Sumatra and Java, appear to have been Telugus. Whilst the Tamil country was overrun by the Telugus in the sixteenth and seventeeth centuries, no corresponding settlement of Tamilians in the Telugu country seems to have taken place. At present, however, most of the Klings found in the Eastern Archipelago are Tamils.

TELUGU GIRL IN FULL DRESS.

One of the names by which the Telugu language is known in the Tamil country is *Vadugu*, from *vada*, north, the Telugu country lying to the north of the Tamil.

The Malas, called Dhers in Gujarat, and Pariahs in the Tamil country, are numerous.

Religion.—Telugu pandits derive the name of their language from *Trilinga*, the language of three lingas, that is, as they represent, of the country of which three celebrated linga temples constituted the boundaries. The majority appear to be Saivas, but towards Orissa, Jagannath is worshipped.

Protestant Christian Missions were not commenced in the Telugu country till 1806, and for a number of years there were very few missionaries. In 1881 the number of Telugu Protestant Christians was about 17,000. They have since greatly increased.

Literature.—The earliest writer on Telugu Grammar is said to have been a sage, called Kanva, who lived at the Court of Andhra-raya, the king in whose reign Sanskrit is said to have been first introduced into the Telugu country. The oldest extant work in grammar (which is composed, like most Telugu grammars, in Sanskrit) was written by a Brahman, called Nannappa, who is also said to be the author of the greater part of the Telugu version of the Mahabharata, the oldest extant composition of any length in Telugu.

Nannappa lived in the reign of Vishnu Vardhana, a king of the Kalinga branch of the Chalukya family, who reigned at Rajamundry about the beginning of the 12th century A.D. Appa-kavi, who ranks next to Nannappa as a grammarian, wrote his Commentaries not in Sanskrit but in Telugu verse.

With the exception of a few works composed towards the end of the 12th century, nearly all the Telugu works that are now extant appear to have been written in the 14th and subsequent centuries, after the establishment of the kingdom of Vijayanagar; and many of them were written in comparatively recent times.

There is a large collection of popular Telugu aphorisms on religious and moral subjects by Vemana: more than 2000 go by his name. They are strongly monotheistic, anti-Brahmanical, and anti-ceremonial. He is supposed to have lived about the 16th century. In style his verses do not differ from the popular compositions of the present day.

Printing commenced among the Telugus in 1806, but made little progress till 1830. About 1835 some Telugu poems were printed in Madras.

KOIS.

The Kois, on the banks of the Upper Godavari, have a tradition that about 200 years ago they were driven down from Bastar. They are supposed to belong to the same race as the Khonds; but a separate account will be given of them.

The Kois generally marry when of a fair age, but infant marriages are not unknown. One form of marriage is that of causing the woman to bend her head down, and then having the man lean over her, the friends pouring water on his head, and when the water has run off his head to that of the woman, they are regarded as man and wife. The water is generally poured out of a bottle-gourd. A Koi, as a rule, will not stir far from his home without one of them filled with water.

The bodies of children and young women are buried. If a child dies within a month of its birth, it is usually buried close to the house, so that the rain dropping from the eaves may fall upon the grave, and thereby cause the parents to be blessed with another child in due course of time. With the above exceptions, corpses are usually burnt. A cow or a bullock is slain and the tail cut off and put in the dead person's hand, after the cotton on which the corpse is carried has been placed upon the funeral pile. After the body has been burnt, the friends retire to feast upon the animal slain for the occasion. Three days afterwards they generally return bringing contributions of grain, and having slain one or more animals, have a second feast.

The general idea of the Kois is that the spirits of the dead wander about the forest in the form of *pishachas*. They do not believe that any one dies what is commonly

KOIS OF UPPER GODAVARI.

called a natural death; but always assert that the death of every one is caused by the machinations of a sorcerer, instigated thereto by an enemy of the deceased or of the deceased's friends. So, in former years, inquiry was always made as to the person likely to have been at such enmity to the deceased as to wish for his death; and having settled upon a suspicious individual, the friends of the deceased used to carry the corpse to the accused, and call upon him to clear himself by undergoing the ordeal of dipping his hands in boiling oil or water. Reputed wizards and witches are held in great abhorrence, and at times the British rule is complained of as unjust in not allowing these people to be put to death.

The goddess Mamile or Lele must be propitiated early in the year, or else the crops will undoubtedly fail; and she is said to be very partial to human victims. Men are occasionally murdered as offerings to this *Devata*; and there is no reason to doubt that every year strangers are quietly put out of the way in the Bastar country to ensure the favour of this blood-thirsty goddess.

Wild dogs are regarded as the messengers of the Pandava brothers. On no account would they attempt to kill one of them, even though it should happen to attack their favourite calf.*

A Christian Mission has been established among the Kois at Dummagudem on the Upper Godavari, and a few have become Christians.

The following is a specimen of the Koi language:—

Nanna tédi, nà, tappénagga anji, ó yaipà, nan na Dévuni munne ní munne pàpam tungi minnàna.—(*Luke* xv. 18.)

ANDAMANESE.

The Andamans are situated in the Bay of Bengal, about 160 miles south of Burma. They consist of three islands,

* From a paper by the Rev. J. Cain in *The Indian Antiquary*, 1876, pp. 357—359.

each about 50 miles in length, with a number of small islands. The Little Andamans lie about 30 miles south of the larger group. They are covered with dense vegetation; but there is an absence of animal life. When discovered, the pig, rat and mungoose were the only quadrupeds. The seas, however, abound with fish, and turtle are plentiful.

ANDAMANESE.

The great interest of the Andamanese is that they are perhaps the only remaining pure specimens of a race of small stature, dark colour, and frizzly hair, which appear to have been the earliest inhabitants of India, South-Eastern Asia, and the islands of the Eastern Archipelago. Traces of them are still found at various spots, but always in the most mountainous and inaccessible regions. The name *negrito*, little negro, has been given to them.

One of the distinctive features of the Andamanese is their small size. The average height of the women is three cubits; that of the men about three inches more. The colour of their skin is almost black, their heads are of the short round type, and their hair is exceedingly closely curled.

The Andamanese go nearly naked, the only clothing being a sort of girdle of leaves. Of the ornaments worn none are more extraordinary than the skulls of deceased relatives, carried suspended from the neck. They also smear themselves with red earth.

They do not cultivate the ground nor keep any domestic animals; but they have a rude kind of hand-made pottery, and make vessels for holding water out of the hollow stems of bamboos; they also make excellent fishing nets and baskets. They are perfect swimmers and divers, and expert at managing canoes. An Andamanese will spring into the water and come up with a fish in each hand. Their principal weapon is the bow and arrow. Their arrow-heads were made of chipped flint, like those in the picture on page 2. They also use spears, harpoons, &c. Before Europeans came to the islands, they had no metals. They live chiefly on wild pigs, turtle, fish, wild fruits, roots, larvæ of insects and honey.

If an Andamanese wants a home, he bends the branches of a tree down to the ground and crawls into the booth he has made. If he needs a grave, his friends bind the branches up, and tying them together, lay and leave his lifeless body among them. Hence, after a time, they obtain the human bones they carry with them as ornaments. Widows have as their special decoration the skulls of their husbands. In the Little Andamans, however, round huts are made large enough to contain 100 persons.

Mourning for deceased relatives consists in shaving, and covering the body from head to foot with a coating of white clay. Their only conception of God is that of an evil spirit who spreads disease.

A convict settlement on the islands was commenced by the Bengal Government in 1789, but it was afterwards given

ANDAMANESE WITH SKULL.

up. The present convict settlement was formed in 1858 at Port Blair, in the southern island of the Great Andaman group. It now contains about 12,000 convicts.

NICOBARESE.

The Nicobars are a smaller group of islands, to the south of the Andamans. The largest is about 30 miles in length. In some of the islands, forests alternate with plains covered with long grass. Cocoanut trees, not found in the Andamans, are numerous. The domestic animals are dogs, pigs, and a few fowls. Fish and shell-fish abound.

The Nicobarese are of a copper colour, short, with Chinese eyes, small flat noses, large mouths, scanty beard, and straight black hair. Their villages are generally built upon the beach, and consist of 15 or 20 houses, each house containing a family of 20 persons and upwards. Their habitations are raised upon wooden pillars about 10 feet from the ground; they are round, without windows, and covered with thatch. The entry is by a trap-door below, through which the family mount by a ladder, which is drawn up at night.

Fishing forms the chief occupation of the Nicobarese. Their food consists of pigs, poultry, turtle, fish, cocoanuts, yams, fruits, &c. In character they are lazy, cowardly, treacherous, and drunken. They have committed several murders on the crews of European vessels. In several instances they received the crews hospitably, and when the sailors were partaking of refreshment, they suddenly rushed upon them, and killed them before they had time to act in defence.

Girls, married at from 13 to 15 years, choose their own husbands. The Nicobarese never keep more than one wife, but they have no scruple in dismissing her on the slightest pretext and taking another.

With the dead the Nicobarese bury most of his moveable property, and fast for two months, abstaining even from their loved tobacco. At the end of that time they dig up the body, when the widow or mother taking the head in her lap, strips it of all putridity, and the remains are finally consigned to the earth. Believing vaguely in a future life, they hold that the spirit joins the *pretas* or demons to whose mischievous action they ascribe all misfortune, whether fever or unsuccessful fishing. To neutralise evil spirits they have exorcists who pretend to cure the sick by extracting from their bodies the stone or pig's tooth which is said to have caused the sickness.

On certain occasions feasts are held to drive off the demons, partly by gifts, partly by force. While the men and priests sit smoking and drinking silently, the women continue to howl dolefully, as they cut up the gifts for the spirits, and throw the fragments into the sea. Daubed over with oil and red paint, and drunk with toddy, the exorcists advance to the attack. Now they coax and now they fight wildly with the malicious spirits to the chorus of the women's howling, till, at last, after a hand to hand battle, the invisible spirits are carried off to a toy boat, festooned with leaves, previously prepared for them. This the youths tow out to sea, where they leave it and its cargo, and return to the feast and the dance. Locked in a circle, with their arms over each other's shoulders, the men leap up and fall down on their heels to the sound of hideous music.

Last century the Dutch tried to colonize the Nicobars ; but the little colony was soon swept away by fever. In 1869 the islands were annexed by the British Government, chiefly to put down piracy, and prevent the murder of ship-wrecked sailors on the islands. Cocoanuts are the principal article of export.

CONCLUDING REMARKS.

The foregoing pages contain a short account of the principal nations and some of the wild tribes of India. On the whole, the impression left is very painful.

Among a large proportion of the inhabitants of India, demon worship, the superstition of savages, still prevails. This is not confined to jungle tribes, but it extends to many living in towns who have had some education.

Sir Monier Williams justly says:

"There is not an object in heaven or earth which a Hindu is not prepared to worship—sun, moon, and stars; rocks, stocks, and stones; trees, shrubs, and grass; sea, pools, and rivers; his own implements of trade; the animals he finds most useful, the noxious reptiles he fears; men remarkable for any extraordinary qualities—for great valour, sanctity, virtue or even vice; good and evil demons, ghosts, and goblins, the spirits of departed ancestors; an infinite number of semi-human and semi-divine existences, inhabitants of the seven upper and the seven lower worlds—each and all come in for a share of divine honours or a tribute of more or less adoration."

"These be thy gods, O India!" There is, however, one Being whom the Hindu rarely worships—the one true God, the great Creator, Preserver, and Governor of the Universe.

God indignantly said to the Jews in old times: "Thou thoughtest that I was altogether such an one as thyself." It is evident that some of the Hindu gods were conceived by wicked men, taking themselves as models.

Just as the King of England forbids any one from setting himself up as king within his empire, so does God forbid the worship of any other than Himself. This is His first command. He cannot permit the creatures whom He made to rise in rebellion against Himself.

God is both our Father and our King.

The worship of any other is a defiance of God's authority, a declaration that we will not have Him to rule over us. All the guilt that lies in foul rebellion against the mildest and most merciful of earthly monarchs, in disobeying the kindest and grieving the best of fathers, in ingratitude to a generous benefactor; all this evil, multiplied a thousand times, there is in polytheism.

God is self-existent, unchangeable, infinite in power, wisdom, goodness and mercy, spotless in holiness. Who are worshipped in His stead? Senseless blocks,—blind, deaf, and dumb,—beasts, birds, and creeping things, the obscene linga, and supposed deities stained with every vice.

Truly Hinduism is a mixture of sin and folly.

The outlook is both discouraging and encouraging.

It is discouraging, because by far the greater number of men who have received a good English education hypocritically support the superstition which in their heart they despise, thus tending to rivet its fetters upon the ignorant; and, though it may be under the form of pseudo-patriotism, proving the worst traitors to their country.

On the other hand there are encouraging signs.

Gladstone says: "I see that for the last fifteen hundred years Christianity has always marched in the van of all human improvement and civilisation, and it has harnessed to its car all that is great and glorious in the human race."

Its influence has already been felt in India. It has quenched the *sati* fires; it has put an end to human sacrifices and infanticide; it has abolished slavery; it has sought to raise those who were degraded by caste beneath the brutes; it has promoted female education; it has pleaded the cause of the widow.

Indian public opinion is getting more and more enlightened. The abominations of Hinduism, which remained unchallenged for thousands of years, are now beginning to outrage the moral sense even of its adherents, and reform is called for. Others, more enlightened, see that a radical change is necessary, that the whole system is wrong from its foundation; that it is opposed to the two grand doctrines of the Fatherhood of God and the Brotherhood of Man; that it fails to meet our greatest needs—the pardon of sin, holiness of heart, and everlasting happiness in heaven.

The Khasis were formerly like the Garos, Nagas, and other hill tribes, sunk in superstition, without a written language, and entirely uneducated; now thousands of them are Christians; their language has been reduced to writing, and their children are educated. In many villages of Tinnevelly and Travancore the orgies of devil-dancing have been exchanged for the devout worship of the one true God.

In all countries there have been some men like the Indian Charvakas, opposed to religion. Such infidels in England have sought to give educated Hindus the impression that Christianity is dying out in the West, that it has been given up by intelligent men, and is confined to the lower orders. On the contrary, some of the greatest statesmen, lawyers, and scientists in England, are true Christians, and the progress of missions throughout the world shows that Christianity was never more vigorous.

Its great Founder said, "To the poor the Gospel is preached." By them it has generally been first embraced; the rich, the noble, being engrossed with the pleasures and honours of the world. So it has been in India. Still, among converts there have been men of noble birth, like the late Prince Rama Varma of Cochin, or of high intellectual ability, as the late Rev. Dr. Krishna Mohun Banerjea, the Sanskrit Examiner of the Calcutta University. One of the most eloquent members of the National Congress is a Brahman convert.

Idolatry in this country will surely come to an end. Under other names many of the same gods now worshipped in India were once worshipped in Europe. A like change will follow. The temples of Vishnu and Siva will yet be as deserted as those of Jupiter and Minerva. "The gods that have not made the heavens and the earth, even they shall perish from the earth and from under the heavens."

The ancestors of the Hindus, the English, and other Aryan nations, says Max Müller, "had once the same faith, and worshipped for a time the same supreme Deity under exactly the same name—a name which meant Heaven-Father." The time will yet come when they will again recognise each other as brethren, kneel together at the same footstool, and offer the same grand old prayer, beginning, "Our Father which art in heaven."

Let the reader not be content to float, like a dead fish, with the current of Hindu society, caring only for his ease and the favour of the ignorant and superstitious. Let him rather seek to have a part in the glorious enterprise of elevating the many millions of this great country, the land of his birth.

A beginning should be made with himself. A prayer for light may first be fitly offered: "*O all-wise, all-merciful God and Father, pour the bright beams of Thy light into my soul, and guide me into Thy eternal truth.*" Reflection on past neglect of duty, and the many sins which have been committed in thought, word, and deed, may well draw forth the confession: "Heavenly Father, I have sinned, and am no more worthy to be called Thy son." According to Hinduism, *karma* must have its course, and the doctrine of the Brahmo Samaj is that every sin must be followed by "adequate agonies." On the other hand Christianity teaches that God, in His great love, has provided a Saviour, the Lord Jesus Christ. He also offers to send his Holy Spirit to purify our hearts and fit them for heaven. Space does not permit the doctrines of Christianity to be explained here. Reference can be made to *Short Papers for Seekers after Truth** and especially to the *New Testament.*

The reader's next efforts should be directed to his wife and children, if he has any, and other relatives. The circle should then be gradually widened.

Blessed are those who, by example and precept, are seeking to turn the people of India from demons and dumb idols to the living God. This would lead to every other needed reform. Unhappy are the men, whatever may be their motives, who are actively or passively countenancing idolatry, thus perpetuating the reign of superstition among their countrymen, with all its attendant evils. It has been well said, WHAT IS NOT TRUE IS NOT PATRIOTIC.

May the prayer of Tennyson, applied to India, soon be heard!

"O Father, touch the East and light
The light that shone when Hope was born."

---

* Price 1 Anna. Obtainable from Mr. A. T. Scott, Tract Depôt, Madras.

GREAT INDIAN QUESTIONS OF THE DAY.

1. **The Religious and Moral Teaching of the Bhagavadgita examined.** 8vo., 72 pp., 2 As. Post-free, 2½ As.

2. **Vedic Hinduism and the Arya Samaj.** 8vo., 104 pp., 2½ As.

3. **Vishnu Bhakti.** 8vo., 56 pp., 1½ As. Post-free, 2 As.

4. **Siva Bhakti.** 8vo., 80 pp., 2 As. Post-free, 3 As.

5. **Vedantism Examined.** 8vo., 68 pp., 2 As. Post-free, 2½ As.

6. **Krishna : the Hindu Ideal.** 8vo., 64 pp., 2 As. Post-free, 2½ As.

7. **Yoga.** 8vo., 56 pp., 2 As. Post-free, 2½ As.

8. **The Call of the Twentieth Century to Awakened India: "Ring out the False, Ring in the True."** 8vo., 103 pp., 3 As.

The Series half bound in cloth, Rs. 1-4.

History of Civilization in India. 8vo., 196 pp., 6 As. Post-free, 7½ As.

A Rational Refutation of the Hindu Philosophical Systems. 2nd edition. 8vo., 208 pp., 10 As., post-free.

Philosophic Hinduism. 8vo., 72 pp., 2½ As. Post-free, 3 As.

Studies in the Upanishads. 8vo., 80 pp., 2½ As. Post-free, 3 As.

Transmigration and Karma. 8vo., 60 pp., 2 As. Post-free, 2½ As.

MADRAS CHRISTIAN COLLEGE MAGAZINE REPRINTS.

EACH ¼ ANNA. 25 COPIES, POST-FREE, FOR 4 AS.

1. **The Point of View.** By Rev. L. P. Larsen.
2. **God is Love.** By Rev. H. Gulliford.
3. **"What is Man?"** By Professor Laidlaw.
4. **God is Spirit.** By Rev. T. E. Slater.
5. **The Supremacy of Conscience.** By Rev. W. H. Findlay, M.A.
6. **The Christian Idea of Sin.** By Professor J. S. Banks, D.D.
7. **The Cross of Christ.** By Professor J. A. Beet, D.D.
8. **The Forgiveness of Sins.** By Professor G. G. Findlay, D.D.
9. **The Fatherhood of God.** By Rev. J. H. Maclean, M.A., B.D.
10. **Renewal.** By Professor J. Denney, D.D.

BARROWS LECTURES.

1. **Christianity, the World-wide Religion.** By Rev. Dr. Barrows, of Chicago. 8vo., 188 pp., 4 As. Post-free, 5½ As.
2. **Christian Belief interpreted by Christian Experience.** By President the Rev. C. H. Hall, D.D., of New York. 8vo., 206 pp., 4 As. Post-free, 5½ As.

Letters to an Indian Youth on the Evidences of Christianity. By Rev. Dr. Murray Mitchell. 12mo., 280 pp., 6 As. Post-free, 7 As.

Bushnell's Character of Jesus, with notes by the Rev. T. E. Slater. 18mo., 92 pp., 1¼ As.

PAPERS FOR THOUGHTFUL HINDUS.

No. 1. The Relation between Christianity and Hinduism. 8vo. 32 pp. By the REV. DR. KRISHNA MOHUN BANERJEA, ½ Anna.

No. 2. The Supposed and Real Doctrines of Hinduism, as held by Educated Hindus. 8vo. 32 pp. by the REV. NEHEMIAH (NILAKANTH) GOREH, ½ Anna.

No. 3. Moral Courage. 8vo. 32 pp. ½ Anna.

No. 4. The Importance of Religion. 8vo. 48 pp. ¾ Anna.

No. 5. Christianity, or—What ? 8vo. 16 pp. ¼ Anna. By the REV. H. RICE.

No. 6. The Sense of Sin in the Light of History. A lecture by the REV. F. W. KELLETT, M.A., Madras Christian College. 8vo. 20 pp. ½ Anna.

No. 7. Bishop Caldwell on Krishna and the Bhagavad Gita. 8vo. 32 pp. ¾ Anna.

No. 8. The Duties of Educated Young Men to their Country. 8vo. 16 pp. ½ Anna.

No. 9. Christ the Fulfilment of Hinduism. 8vo. 28 pp. ½ Anna. By the REV. F. W. KELLETT, M.A.

No. 10. Vedantism. 8vo. 21 pp. ½ Anna.

No. 11. The Defectiveness of Brahmoism. 8vo. 24 pp. ½ Anna. Both the preceding are by the REV. LAL BEHARI DAY.

No. 12. Preliminary Dialogues on Important Questions in India. 8vo. 74 pp. 2 As. Post-free, 2½ As.

No. 13. Helps to Truth-Seekers. 8vo. 32 pp. 1 Anna.

No. 14. Hindu Pantheism. 8vo. 18 pp. ½ Anna. By DR. FLINT.

No. 15. Hinduism and Christianity: a Comparison and a Contrast. 8vo. 64 pp. 1½ As. By the REV. DR. J. P. JONES.

No. 16. The Gods of Ancient Europe. 8vo. 80 pp. 2 As. Post-free, 2½ As.

No. 17. The Religious Ideals of the East and West. 8vo. 24 pp. ½ Anna. By the REV. DR. J. P. JONES.

No. 18. Famous Philosophers of Ancient Europe. 8vo. 64 pp. 1½ As.

No. 19. Hindu and Christian Conceptions of God. 8vo. 52 pp. 1 Anna.

No. 20. Hindu and Christian Ideas regarding Sin and its Pardon. 8vo. 26 pp. ½ Anna.

No. 21. True Patriotism. 8vo. 15 pp. ½ Anna.

No. 22. Universal Religion.

M. E. PRESS, MOUNT ROAD, MADRAS, 1908.

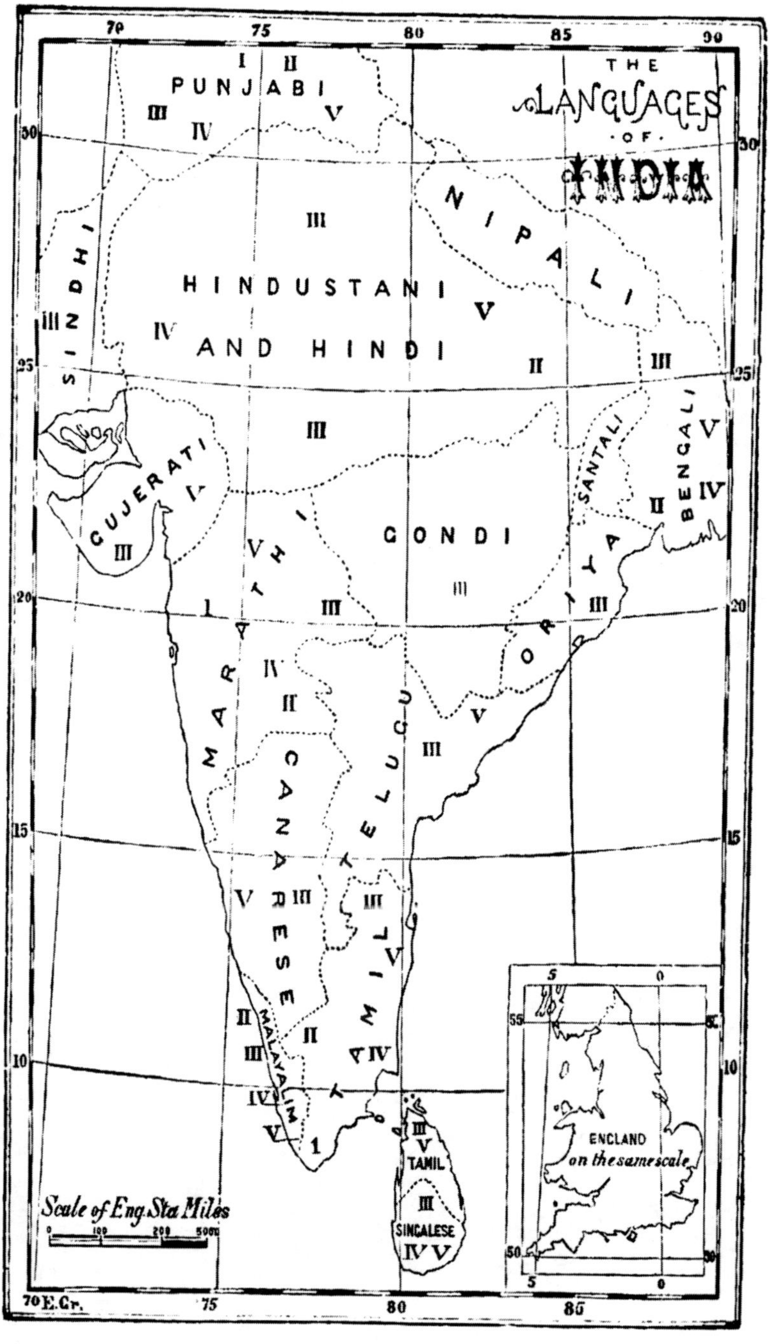

LANGUAGE MAP OF INDIA.